T0333387

Textiles are a great source of inspiration and narrative. Through the physical medium of fabric, stories can be made intimate.

Having a story to tell often starts and underpins a work of art's design process. In this fascinating book, Cas Holmes shows how inspiration can be found in the world around us – from seasonal changes in the surrounding landscape, or the urban detritus on our street. Building a connection to familiar places or subjects of interest is a vital means for seizing inspiration and developing stories. This inspiring book shows you how to record your experiences, using sketchbooks, journals and photography to create personal narratives that can form a starting point for more finished stitched-textile pieces.

This book progresses from an exploration into different methods of recording ideas and inspiration, to a practical guide on how to translate your ideas onto fabric and use expert techniques to add more interest to your work. The potential for using textiles to stitch your own stories is limitless, and this book helps you take inspiration from the world around you to create and develop your own beautiful and unique work.

STITCH
STORIES

STITCH STORIES

STORIES

Personal places, spaces and traces in textile art

CAS HOLMES

BATSFORD

First published in the United Kingdom
in 2015 by Batsford

43 Great Ormond Street
London WC1N 3HZ

An imprint of B. T. Batsford Holdings
Limited

Copyright © B. T. Batsford Ltd 2015
Text © Cas Holmes 2015

All rights reserved. No part of this
publication may be copied, displayed,
extracted, reproduced, utilized,
stored in a retrieval system or
transmitted in any form or by any
means, electronic, mechanical or
otherwise including but not limited to
photocopying, recording, or scanning
without the prior written permission
of the publishers.

ISBN: 9781849942744

A CIP catalogue record for this book
is available from the British Library.

10 9

Reproduction by COLOURDEPTH, UK
Printed by Toppan Leefung Printing
Ltd, China

This book can be ordered direct
from the publisher at the website
www.batsfordbooks.com, or try your
local bookshop.

Page 2 Cas Holmes, *Snowdrop* 2014,
27 x 27cm (10½ x 10½in). The image
of the snowdrops on the vintage
cigarette card is echoed in the
free-machine stitch drawing.

Contents

Right *Great Tapestry of Scotland*. Designed by Andrew Crummy. Stitch co-ordinator Dorie Wilkie. One of 164 panels totalling 1 x 124m (1 x 155yd). Image based on Charles Rennie Mackintosh's design for the Glasgow School of Art. Wool embroidered on to linen. 100 x 10cm (39 x 39in).

Introduction: finding inspiration for textile art

It is not often that you come across an artist that plays between the worlds of man and nature. Most find inspiration either in one or the other; we are all familiar with textile work that holds urbanity or nature as its core inspiration. However, Cas Holmes has found a third way, the point where both touch, not collide, but touch. This haunted land full of 'the shadows of marks made by man in the earth', of 'reflections in water and flooded fields', of 'gardens and seasons changing', is one that is often missed by the passer-by and artist alike, but it is a rich and rewarding place. It is an inspirational well of harmony and balance, as well as of conflict and division. Something shared and something complementary, as she says herself:

'We have an intimate relationship with the land, but equally share "common connection".'

Cas helps others to search and explore the world of the found and the displaced, the cast aside, or perhaps just the mislaid. It is a rich vein of potential and a revelation of connections between … our human world … [and] the world we refer to as natural.

(JOHN HOPPER 2014)

I use textiles and found materials with a connection to the things I find interesting when encountered during my daily activities and places visited as part of my working and social life. My Romany grandmother fostered this interest in the reclaimed – the often overlooked 'things' found along the sides of a path, road or field. In Romany culture, these 'things' had practical uses: for example willow was made into pegs, and reeds and rushes into baskets. My love of storytelling was inherited from her, and I remember her entertaining me with stories of her childhood travelling.

My father has influenced me too. When I was a schoolgirl, I regularly accompanied him on his walk home from work. He encouraged me to look around and to ask questions about the things we observed on these walks: the plaster decorations above eye level on the medieval buildings in the city streets, the shape of a tree against a winter landscape, or the simple breaking through of the first snowdrops or bluebells in our local wood.

I like to 'do different', as we say in Norfolk, and find different ways of exploring my ideas. I am still interested in the commonplace, things observed on the edges of our vision, and my connection to cloth as an artist and teacher has enriched my investigations. I spent four years at art college, training in painting and drawing, but soon became involved with the world of stitch. Paradoxically, my own works have since been described as 'painting with cloth'. I work without defined boundaries, cutting, tearing, painting and sewing cloth as I trace a personal response to the historical, environmental and social heritage of a place and create new meanings within my work.

A social fabric

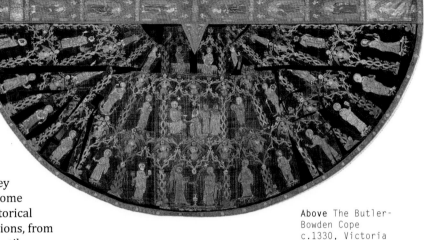

Above The Butler-Bowden Cope c.1330, Victoria and Albert Museum.

Textiles are the social fabric of our cultural history. Everyday stitched textiles for domestic use, where they have survived, remind us of our family connections. Some of us still use items that have been handed down. Historical pieces housed in museums and National Trust collections, from the richly embroidered gowns of the wealthy to the textile hangings for walls and beds, reflect our shared history and remind us of the significance and value of textiles as a symbol of status, comfort and wealth.

The idea that cloth and stitch can be used to communicate a story is not new. Surviving examples of Opus Anglicanum (English work) embroidery, which were mostly designed for liturgical use in the form of copes and vestments, described narratives from the Bible in visual form. These exquisite and expensive pieces of medieval embroidery, of which few survive, contained complex decorative motifs such as flowers, animals, birds, beasts and angels, as well as figures of the saints and biblical characters, all heavily embroidered in gold and silver thread and rich silks. Such was the importance of this art form in medieval England that BBC4 dedicated an hour of prime-time television to a discussion on Opus Anglicanum. In his introduction the programme, presenter Dan Jones (2013) described the quality of stitch in the Butler-Bowden Cope housed in the collection at the Victoria and Albert Museum: 'It is almost as if this whole piece has been signed with a needle "This is from England" ', and further comments: 'The English elevated the craft of embroidery into an art of stunning realism and emotion.'

The use of stitch remains at the centre of our lives today. At the same time as the referendum was being held over the question of Scottish independence in 2014, the Great Tapestry of Scotland was being exhibited in the Scottish Parliament buildings. The brainchild of the author Alexander McCall Smith and historian Alistair Moffat, the tapestry was designed by Andrew Crummy and work on its illustrated panels was carried out by over 1,000 volunteer embroiderers in one of Scotland's largest community projects. It follows in a grand tradition of stitching narratives: the Bayeux Tapestry, depicting the conquest of England by William Duke of Normandy in 1066 at the Battle of Hastings, is the most well known of the genre.

Artists continue to use cloth for reasons beyond its practical qualities. It ties us to the past and reflects upon the present. Sue Prichard, curator of textiles at the Victoria and Albert Museum, talks about this intimacy and the intriguing relationship she has had with cloth since childhood, when her grandmother taught her to knit and sew:

Domestic textiles are very important to me. My first sewing box was made of cheap, brightly coloured cardboard but I loved that box with a passion and it was the first thing I turned to when I arrived home from school. I made table mats, chair-back covers, needle cases, pincushions – all from scraps and mostly from my grandmother's fabric stash. I would gift these items to various members of my family, but nobody appreciated them as much as my grandmother. She worked as a domestic cleaner in a large house in Chelsea as well as running her own home, but always took pleasure in sitting down at the end of the day with her needle. My life differs from my grandmother's on so many levels; however, I always find time to connect to my past. Now I have many sewing boxes in the sitting room, bedroom and kitchen – all filled with my grandmother's needles, pincushions, scissors and hundreds of buttons, all recycled and kept for a rainy day.
(SUE PRICHARD IN A LETTER TO CAS HOLMES, JULY 2014)

She further explains how the V&A has had a lasting influence on her work:

The V&A has always been my local museum. My grandmother brought me here when I was a child and I remember wanting to walk through the doors marked 'Staff Only'. I was intrigued by what lay behind. That thought's still important and informs my work.

(SUE PRICHARD IN AN ARTICLE 'DOMESTIC GODDESS', *EMBROIDERY MAGAZINE*, MAY/JUNE 2014)

As we handle cloth and learn from others, we equally become aware of the story woven into its making.

In this book

This book builds on the design ideas and creative processes briefly discussed in the chapter 'Magpie of the Mind' in my book *The Found Object in Textile Art*, and takes a closer look at how the everyday and the familiar can be a starting point for developing ideas. We look at connections to places and subjects of interest as a means of developing stories or narratives in stitch and cloth. There are ideas for practical projects linking techniques to concept, supported by examples of work from some of the leading practitioners and artists in textiles.

In chapter 1, 'Places, Spaces and Traces', we consider approaches to keeping a journal or a sketchbook and other methods for recording ideas. Collected materials are a starting point for development, and we can explore the qualities inherent in them. There are practical exercises to help you translate ideas into cloth, mixed media and stitch.

For suggestions on how to come up with ideas, look at chapter 2, 'Seizing Inspiration', which explores traditional and unusual sources. Chapter 3, 'The Natural World', shows that the world we live in can be a rich resource for our creativity, from the detritus of urban backyards and gardens to seasonal changes in the landscape.

'All in the Detail', chapter 4, looks at how works can be imbued with a wealth of rich detail in order to be read on a number of levels, and also covers printing techniques and making book forms. Chapter 5, 'Off the Beaten Path', looks at responses to personal themes and interests, the history and properties of cloth and stitch as a resource, and artists' interactions and comments on historical and social narratives. Chapter 6 continues this theme but focuses on the possibilities of hand stitching, in 'Telling Stories in Stitch'.

Interwoven into the chapters are a variety of processes and techniques that you can adapt to your own creative approaches so you too can 'do different'.

Opposite Detail of a winter tree in a paper collage with ink colours and drawing on top.

9

PLACES, SPACES AND TRACES

At some point, all artists need to find their own approach to their subject matter, enabling them to make work that is meaningful to them and produces an individual take on the world. The motivation behind our desire to make things is as relevant as the way we make them. For me, journeys strike a particular chord. Travel takes place in the mind as much as across land or even continents. The anticipation of a journey not only prepares me for what is to come but is also sweet with expectation about what I might do on arrival. I use the time spent travelling to think, and to make connections between my home territory and the destination. I collect materials, take photographs, and make notes and sketches to record what I see. Your artistic take on the world could be sparked by your daily journey to work, seasonal changes in your garden, family stories, local history, or even an intuitive response to the feel and history of a piece of cloth. Such things provide a rich resource in developing your own narratives, or what some may call a personal vision.

Stitch-sketching

When the woman you live with is an artist, every day is a surprise. Clare has turned the second bedroom into a wonder cabinet, full of small sculptures and drawings pinned up on every inch of wall space. There are coils of wire and rolls of paper tucked into shelves and drawers. The next day I come home to find that Clare has created a flock of paper and wire birds, which are hanging from the ceiling in the living room. A week later our bedroom windows are full of abstract blue translucent shapes that the sun throws across the room onto the walls, making a sky for the bird shapes Clare has painted there. It's beautiful.

AUDREY NIFFENEGGER, *THE TIME TRAVELER'S WIFE*

Developing a vision

The activity of drawing and recording my daily observations, and the realization of some of those ideas in textiles, is a process I call 'stitch-sketching'. I have spent considerable time thinking through ideas and developing the processes behind them, both as an artist and as a teacher.

The act of drawing informs rather than 'directs' my ideas in cloth and is an important part of my reflective practice. The mechanics of making a mark differ as well. A drawn line is 'surface bound' – it is largely worked on to (and bites into) the surface of the paper or canvas ground and usually lacks any relief. Work in stitch requires it to be worked through the front and the back of the material, giving a texture to the cloth or paper. This direct interaction of thread, needle and material creates its own vocabulary of marks, which is unique to the feel and the look of the work.

On the relationship between drawing and stitch, Nigel Hurlstone (2010) refers to 'the potential of [machine] embroidery to create a new and different language that does not duplicate the original source, but breathes into it a different life that celebrates the haptic qualities of stitch and the unpredictability of cloth and thread as a way to leave an imprint of thought, time, process and the hand of the maker on and within a surface.'

The refining of processes and approach requires practice, through which you can learn to develop your ideas and portray them in a way that is unique to you. Looking around you, making notes, taking photographs and drawing in a sketchbook are great ways of developing your vision, but you also need to master textile skills and develop stitch techniques to bring your ideas to fruition. Learn all the techniques that interest you, but don't be afraid to experiment, adapt processes and make mistakes – failed experiments are time well spent. Work without fear and push yourself creatively so that you can spot opportunities where you would not normally expect to find them.

Equipment and materials

Over many years of travel and being on the road (without a car), I have learned to carry the bare minimum. If I forget something, I make do or improvise. I will exchange and dispose of resources – such as found objects, fragments of cloth and paper – as they catch my eye. Limiting what you use to what can easily be carried is a useful creative tool. Materials and tools are as individual as the artist who compiles them, and often reflect the character and nature of his/her work. I carry the following items in a small, portable kit whenever I am away for more than a day or two:

• Small sketchbook or journal – and on the rare occasions that I don't have one with me, I improvise with found paper collected en route, which you can do too.

• Selection of pens, wax crayons, pencils, water-based paint, small brushes, glue stick, rubber bands (to hold pages down) and a medicine bottle to use as a water pot.

• A viewfinder (an old picture-frame window mount, slide mount, or envelope windows can make good alternatives).

• Scissors, scalpel, 15cm (6in.) steel ruler.

• Stitching kit kept in a small textile pouch: needles, small selection of threads and scissors.

• A point-and-shoot camera.

• Tablet or phone for reviewing work.

I carried the above kit around Australia and the USA and it was sufficient for most of my teaching projects.

Left Portable sewing kit against the background of a work in progress. I carry this along with a travelling sketchbook and drawing kit kept in a small clutch bag.

Back home

(166)

Friday 20th Sept 2013

I'm creating a blog post on gardening for an RHS competition. And I suddenly had the idea of using seed-packets, napkins, maps and stitching; plus painted muslin.

Hanging for zigzag book? Whichever, use linen binding for hinges.

front —

cheesecloth

reverse

Paint the cheesecloth (fuse with gel medium, and lightly brush thinned white acrylic over seed-packet image.

Napkins - apply to maps with acrylic wax, then stitch around the shapes.

map + napkins

Photos taken of packet sequence. → 13 11 10 9 / 8 7 6 5 / 4 3 2 1 ←

Title? Possibly 'Seed Packet Mapped Treasures'

(167)

Monday 23rd Sept 2013

Much achieved over the weekend: seed-packets selected, words written for them and for the inner napkin pages: twelve of each - a concertina book.

Maps cut (12 + 2 for trials), napkin motifs likewise, and all adhered using acrylic wax. As the wax dries, the napkins become transparent - the map is still visible. Fuse maps & packets to muslin.

word / herb / veg

salad

Now to type and print the words on the layout paper stained with teabags. Iron to Bondaweb, cut & stitch in place. (See notes for positioning)

Now create hinges using calico (oversize, trim afterwards and position between one set of pages. Turn the zigzag over, and position the reverse. Stitch around each page in two strips.

(trim) → accurately.

Right Ann Somerset Miles, *Mapping Seed Packet Treasures*, 2013. This project began as part of Ann's gardening blog: 'The thought of the wonderful plants you can grow from tiny seeds inspired what was going to be a simple zigzag booklet. But once started, the creative aspect took over and it has become double-sided - 12 seed-packet panels on one side, and 12 map panels on the other side.'

A journal: recording process

It is a richly rewarding experience to develop a sketchbook or journal and you can work in it in a number of ways. You may require solitude, time and quiet as your work evolves, or prefer to work with others in a small group as part of an experimental approach. Journals can be undertaken to record travel, new experiences, or to research a design aspect for a new project.

The sharing of studies digitally, through forums and blogs, can be a useful way of discussing ideas and getting feedback on your work. There are many online certificated courses in textiles, as well as informal workshop blogs which allow for the exchange of practical skills needed for developing sketchbooks and creative textile ideas.

A diverse range of media, materials and methods can be used to record your ideas. Drawing, print, diagrams, photographs, images, text, journals, indexes, dictionaries, mind mapping and many other approaches form part of the artist's tools for exploring and communicating complex visual ideas. Keeping a record, creating a journal or recording in a sketchbook as part of a reflective process is a valuable part of your creativity.

An artist's journal

Ann Somerset Miles works from her studio in the roof space of her Cotswold farmhouse and, when travelling, on a tiny table in her caravan. She is also a prodigious journalist:

I manage to get to my worktable on most days and am continually experimenting with techniques new to me, or creating samples for one of the numerous fabric/paper journals that are always in the pipeline. Samples are filed in stackable boxes or loose-leaf folders alongside copies of notes from my sketchbooks. I love to say 'What if?' and not be afraid of failure – though even the rejects are repurposed.

Jane LaFazio

Jane LaFazio is a mixed-media artist and teacher working in paper and cloth. She lives in San Diego, California, USA. She discovered her ability to draw when her beloved husband had a serious illness, requiring her to become a full-time carer for a while, explaining:

I was losing the 'Jane' in me, while grieving my husband's cognitive losses from his acquired brain injury and the future plans we'd made. I signed up for a drawing class, every Tuesday morning. I realized I could draw!

As Jane's work evolved, she embraced the Internet and social-media platforms, recognizing the role they could play in the sharing and exchanging of ideas. She blogs frequently about her creative pursuits, sharing tutorials and pages from her sketchbook, or reflecting on recent trips that have provided her with inspiration.

Her subject matter is the things she observes regularly, including the eucalyptus trees prevalent in the local area, as she reveals:

There are many types of eucalyptus trees, some with long, thin leaves with shades of blue, green, red and purple. Other varieties sprout lovely pods, and soon those pods open to brilliant pink silky floss. As I walk in my neighbourhood, I often bring home a leaf, blossom or pod to draw in my sketchbook.

I do what I describe as 'designs from life', where I will draw and paint the subject as realistically as I can in the time I have. Then, inspired by the shapes I've just drawn, I let my imagination take over and reference my drawings to make simple graphic designs to use in the creation of a hand-carved stamp, a rubbing, a stencil or a silkscreen.

Below Jane LaFazio, *Eucalyptus Blooms*, 2013. Free-motion drawing with sewing machine on to fabric printed with thermofax screens and stencils of the blossom. A three-dimensional element was added with blossom worked with Lutradur and 'strings' of fabric machine-zigzag stitched into cords. **Above** Drawings of the blooms in progress.

A sketch in time

When I pull out a sketchbook or journal and look back at my studies, I am taken to a specific place and time. The studies reflect the points at which I have stopped and looked, particularly when travelling. The drawings and accompanying notes give a better recollection of that experience, or place, than any photograph. Equally, changes in time and weather, shifting light, and a sense of place become embedded in the journal as part of the process of recording. I glue various small items collected from the locality into the pages, make rubbings and prints from leaves and seasonal plants, and record the shifting light and patterns seen in the landscape in the colours and textures used in the drawings.

Hunting and gathering

Log your progress in whatever ways feel suitable: in a notebook, a sketchbook, on a wall in your studio, on digital media or by using a combination of all these. I still like to carry a small sketchbook and pen whenever I can, but will often take a quick snap with my phone, or make notes on my tablet of things of interest. I often refer to this part of my process as 'hunting and gathering', and carry a small bag to collect items to use.

Sometimes I search for specific things for a project or commission; at other times, I just gather ideas along the way as I travel. When I stop for a break or to take in a view, or even while waiting for public transport, I find somewhere I can sit comfortably for 20 minutes (or stand if necessary) to create a quick impression of something that catches my eye. I usually work directly with pen for ease of use, but you can also draw a loose sketch with a pencil first and then use a permanent fine-point pen to refine and redraw, and then erase the pencil. Alternatively, water-soluble pens such as a Berol fine point can produce lovely runs and bleeds. I then apply colour to the drawing from a limited colour palette of watercolour or Koh-I-Noor paints.

Above Sketchbook and samples for the *Norfolk and Netherlands* studies (see page 33) of plants and a stitch-sample landscape.

Below Sketchbook graphic looking at approaches to joining different-shaped pages to create a zigzag book.

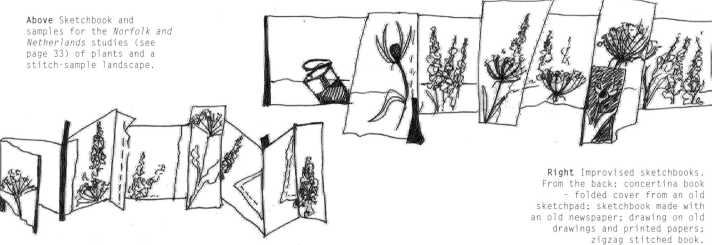

Right Improvised sketchbooks. From the back: concertina book – folded cover from an old sketchpad; sketchbook made with an old newspaper; drawing on old drawings and printed papers; zigzag stitched book.

Working methods

Keep this checklist in mind.

• Note down and draw the things of interest you see on a daily basis, and take photographs which can later be added to the journal and/or kept digitally.

• Start a collection based on the first found object/range of objects you see on a daily walk.

• Create a body of theme-related studies using photographs, notes and drawings (maybe a whole sketchbook or journal), simplifying and observing.

• Jot down any words or phrases that come to mind when considering your theme. Poetry, paragraphs from a novel, or pieces of music may connect to the work you have in mind, or be a stimulus for further ideas.

• Record and make samples of your processes when learning a technique. Keep them in a binder or sketchbook, noting your thoughts and sources of inspiration (for example peeling walls, patterns from a building, flora).

• Create your own sketchbooks by stitching (or gluing) different types and weights of paper together. These can be in various colours, or tones (light to dark), and the format of the sketchbook can be of your choosing: square, book-fold, irregular, zigzag or even triangulated.

The musician Leonard Cohen regularly sketches or documents the things he uses or sees as part of his daily routine, as a form of meditative practice, and states: 'I have always loved things, just things in the world. I love trying to find the shape of things.'

Recording with digital media

Digital photography and design software such as Photoshop or PaintShop Pro provide endless creative possibilities for the textile artist. Working from photographs can be difficult, especially when a photograph captures an image successfully, but they are good reminders of things observed and can be used as a design aid to complement your drawings.

I am often asked what the best program and camera to use are. Beyond simple cropping, I rarely use software for editing or changing my photos. I prefer to print images and edit them physically by tearing, cutting and isolating areas of interest, and then working back into the resulting sections with collage and drawing. I have a good digital SLR to record my work as it progresses, but otherwise use a point-and-shoot camera most of the time when travelling. Recognize the limits and capabilities of the equipment you use. I would never document my work with a camera phone or tablet for professional purposes, but find them useful for quick, inspirational snaps to share with friends on social media or to upload to my blog, or for reference in my sketchbooks.

Software packages, photocopiers, tablets and scanners are excellent tools to use for repeating an image and experimenting with patterns, and you can draw directly using picture-editing programs. They can also be used to enlarge segments of drawings to reveal unusual, abstract designs, alter colourways, and layer one image upon another. Whatever level of confidence or experience you may have with digital media, the exercises below can be done manually (after you have printed your images) as well as digitally.

Droplets – reeds – leaves – late Autumn change scale.

Below, from left to right Lea Valley weeds, Medway barge, Oosterschelde in the Netherlands and Valerian on wasteland in Rochester.

Left Isolation studies of plants: collages made with photographs and line drawings of plants.

Below Crow animation in stitch. Turn to the back of the book to animate the crows using your smartphone.

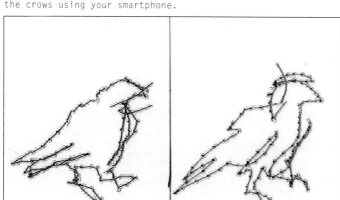

Digital exercises

• Photograph textures of everyday things such as kitchen and household objects, cut up the printed images and glue into collages to make patterns. Make further drawings and designs from these patterns.

• Make a series of photographs of the same or similar subjects, such as small details of plants, interesting walls or reflections in water, for example. Crop and present these in a regular-shaped box or rectangle. This will help you to examine the subject in more detail.

• Enlarge or reduce the size of the image and isolate areas of interest such as the colour, shape, tone or texture.

• Photocopy or print images on top of each other to achieve a layered image.

• Photograph a drawing or collage as it progresses as a means to monitor the changes.

Chance discoveries

Exploiting the possibilities of digital media can lead to new directions in your work. As part of a fundraising event in aid of an Indian charity, I needed to find a way of making a simple repeat and so produced a small print run of a 'Crow' textile in a bookmark form. These were embellished with free-machine stitch to give them an individual feel. Turning the bookmarks over, ready to be attached to handmade paper, revealed a characterful run of 'stitched crow' drawings. I then animated these in a basic stop-frame movie program, creating a moving stitched drawing with sound.

Stitch-sketching is for all

We sometimes worry too much about other people's opinions of the drawings we make. We all have the power of observation and an ability to make a mark. Practice over time enables us to create form and develop our ideas with these marks, just as surely as we create words and sentences with marks on paper. My sketchbooks are not a linear thought process but a means to keep me looking; however, like the heritage of my Norfolk landscape, the notes and observations I make find a way of seeping into my work.

Mark-making

A sketchbook is a means to explore; it is an aid to your own development. When drawing, have visual curiosity, look at everything as if for the first time, see and observe rather than just looking. Creating your own marks for painting on to cloth, or to translate into texture for stitch, is part of experimentation and play:

• Explore different drawing implements such as sticks for use as ink pens, charcoal and wax crayons. Work on top of varied paper surfaces, from lightweight tissue and brown paper to heavy drawing paper and printed matter.

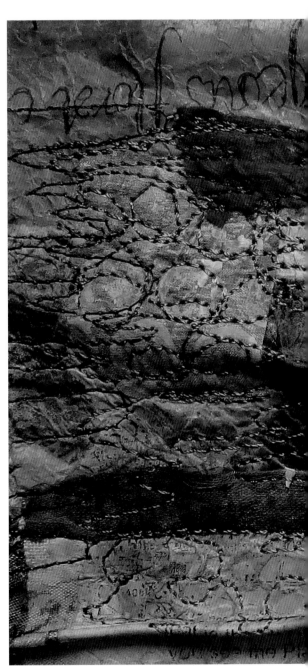

• Experiment with approaches to marking the paper beforehand, using mixed-media techniques such as staining pages with paint, ink or dye, or making a rubbing with pencils or crayons to 'remove' the sometimes offputting blank page.

Below and below left Ros Woodhead, location drawings and textile sample reflecting the landscape of South West France as part of a workshop at Studio Préniac.

• Vary the position of the subject or object and how you look at it, change the scale of the drawing on the page, and look at areas of detail, interesting outlines or the shadows and shapes in changing light.

• Mark boxes on a page and make a textural drawing in each box, reflecting the surfaces and patterns you see around you in natural and man-made forms, from leaves and plants to weathered walls and drain covers.

Below Kate Boucher, design board with
samples and ideas relating to plants
and landscape as part of workshops at
West Dean Summer School.

Below Various sketchbooks illustrating
the stitched book below made from
the cover of a drawing pad and other
extended drawing books.

- Change the shape of drawings: make them long, vertical, circular or square. These could provide useful references and formats for collage and stitch composition.
- Create three-dimensional drawings. Cut, fold, crease, concertina and crumple pages.
- Lay out different papers (such as drawing paper, brown paper, newspaper, wallpaper and watercolour paper) along the length of a table, overlapping and changing their orientation as you work. Tear some of the edges of the paper and allow your drawing to travel across the pages as you overlap the working sketches and layer them.
- Stitch directly into your sketchbook, attach pages where needed, tear and add pages to others. (I often find it easier to stitch an extension to a page rather than use glue.)
- Isolate areas of research drawings you have made, using viewfinders or a camera, and create a series of studies from these 'isolations'.
- Scale up drawings and isolations. You can do this by scanning and enlarging sections on a computer, or by tracing the image on to acetate sheets with pens and then projecting the enlarged tracing (with an overhead projector) on to your chosen paper and/or cloth surface attached to a board or wall.

Above Sketchbook with
extended and stitched pages.
Norfolk Weeds series.

Tania McCormack

Left Tania McCormack, *School*, 2004. Image on the back of a postcard with hand stitch and pen drawing.

The boundaries between drawing, painting and stitch can become blurred as you work and select each medium as appropriate to the task in hand. Artist Tania McCormack makes drawings, prints and work in stitch according to the qualities and narratives she is seeking in her work. Most of her drawings are made on location and reference daily journeys connecting people to place. She explains:

I enjoy recording what I overhear, see and experience overall in my work, creating a storyline. Architectural details, conversations, found items on pavements, shop signage... a general recording of a place including 'grotty parts' in which I find beauty.

Investigative in approach, Tania concentrates on details, changes scale and overlaps her drawings and prints as she works. She regards this journalistic approach as essential to her work, and uses a sketchbook as a visual diary, adding layers of 'history' as she moves around. She produced a series of small, stitched travelcards and location drawings on tea-stained postcards for an exhibition called 'E9 – Anatomy of an Area'. Based on a culmination of journeys made on foot around the small area of London in the E9 postcode, the pieces were originally inspired by beautifully embroidered wartime postcards. Tania elaborates:

I found it sad that these items were discarded in a secondhand/ antiques shop and I wondered about the owner and the stories behind them. This motivated me to make the same connections when I started collecting used paper and found travelcards as I moved around London. I liked the use of stitch at this point as a different medium and what it brought to the pieces. It seemed to be able to say more than if I had used paint, for example.

SEIZING
INSPIRATION

Working with stitch on to cloth is only part of
the process of developing your narrative. You can
'seize inspiration' from resources that form part of
your working day. The objects you collect - printed
materials, old wallpaper books, even a grain of
rice - can provide starting points for your ideas.
Traditional or unusual, this section looks at the
different approaches you can take to develop your
ideas and move them into another dimension.

Memory museums

We all collect objects, postcards and images, and enjoy favourite pieces of writing or music in some form or another. These all have the power to generate wonder, evoke a memory, and act as reminders of places visited. I refer to my collections as 'memory museums' and just as in a museum, I reorganize them, put some away and look at them afresh as I work. Notes from a museum or gallery visit, a group of objects, or a favourite book or poem can all be a rich source of ideas. The sculptor Henry Moore collected seashells, bones, pebbles and various other found objects, using them as 'natural sculptures' and sources of inspiration for his work.

You can organize your 'museum' as physical objects for reference, as a collection of photographs, or make notations in your sketchbook/ notebook (or any combination of methods). I sometimes lose sight of where I 'catalogued' and stored a particular object or memory, and then when I open up a small box or an old sketchbook I find a link to my current work and rediscover another approach worthy of reinvestigation.

Left Sketchbook study of fish by June Jordan. Painted and photographic studies and exploration on crumpled paper backgrounds.

Inspiring wallpaper

My father, a painter and decorator, brought home wonderful wallpaper sample books and paint charts from our local hardware and decorating shop which I cut up to make collages. I became familiar with the colours and patterns of twentieth-century design for domestic interiors and homes through glimpses of these wonderful wallpapers before I fully appreciated their origins. On rare trips to London with my father, we visited the Victoria and Albert Museum. This was where I saw some of the designs for wallpaper and cloth by William Morris and members of the Arts & Crafts Movement, accessed through a wonderful collection of viewing drawers.

I also discovered shining, ornate glass, and ceramic and silver objects in dark-wood display cases in dimly lit rooms. I fondly remember a glass vase painted in enamel with a rich tracery of leaf patterns, reminding me of the elegance of the waterside grasses of my native Norfolk. The piece, a carafe designed by Richard Redgrave (1804–88), was called Well Spring and was typical of the design work of the Arts & Crafts Movement. This interest in looking at historical design examples opened up my passion for exploring the natural world as a subject and as an inspirational source.

Later, when teaching at Middlesex University, I became familiar with the Silver Studio collection at the Museum of Domestic Design and Architecture and was able to revisit some of the wallpaper patterns I remembered as a child. The studio, founded by Arthur Silver in 1880, produced some of the best-known fabric, wallpaper, carpet and metalwork designs for companies such as Liberty's, Sanderson, and Warner and Sons, well into the late twentieth century. Many of these designs are still in use today. Both the Victoria and Albert Museum and the Museum of Domestic Design and Architecture have a good online gallery of their collections and related reference materials. The Museum of Art and Design in New York, the Musée des Arts Décoratifs in Paris, and many other internationally renowned museums also have inspiring collections. Your local museum, art gallery or library can be equally stimulating as a resource for visual inspiration.

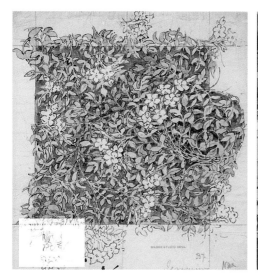

Above A design for a textile, carpet or wallpaper by the Silver Studio, c.1890. The design features coils of jasmine with a closely patterned ground of leaves.

Above An Art Nouveau design by the Silver Studio for wallpaper featuring a flower in the fashionable aesthetic colours of the period. The design was sold to Wylie & Lochhead and became known as the 'Rokesley Poppy'. This type of wallpaper pattern was very popular in smart middle-class drawing rooms in the early 1890s.

Above A drawing by Cas Holmes of *Well Spring*, a vase designed by Richard Redgrave.

Design ideas from printed materials

I still collect wallpaper samples and paint charts and use the coloured squares as a teaching resource. Isolated areas of interest cut out from coloured postcards and design magazines also work well as colour research design tools. Large rolls of plain wallpaper or lining paper are ideal for collaborative drawing and painting sessions, or as backgrounds to view your work. Textured wallpaper is great for taking rubbings. Try the following suggestions to experiment with these resources:

• Create collages based on two to three colour ranges cut from paint charts or from sections of postcards or magazines. Explore different colour combinations such as analogous colours (e.g. blue/purple) or complementary colours (e.g. yellow/purple).

• Create different marks with rubbings, drawings and prints on a length of wallpaper. Either work on your own, or in a small group, rotating the paper around as you work. Working with other people encourages interaction and experimentation with the marks and also removes the responsibility of ownership from the design.

• Scan or photograph parts of collages or drawings, or isolate small areas of interest with a viewerfinder, and use these as a starting point for further design development.

• Find colours in the world around you that relate to those on the paint chart, making notes of where you saw the colours, and then rename the colour charts with these new names.

Colour notes

Our perception of colour is complex and based upon our own experiences and memory. We identify objects and scenes and give them meaning by the use of universally accepted colours – for example green grass, or blue sky. However, we have the freedom to change the norms of colour, which allows us to see content in a more abstract or expressive context. Colour is always moving and changing; it is never fixed. Working with a collection of colours and keeping a colour notebook allows you to explore new combinations and broadens your colour palette; observations of the real world will feed into this to enrich your colour usage in your work.

  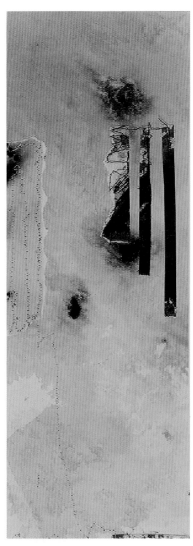

Above,left and right
Printed and marked
collection of paper
and fabrics from a
collaborative mark-making
exercise using pen, ink
and wash. These were then
used for collages and
stitched in compositions
during a workshop at
Studio Préniac, France.

Right Paint-card samples.
Colours cut from these
cards were used to
explore colour themes
around the idea for a
collage called *Grass is
Greener* (see also pages
32 and 47).

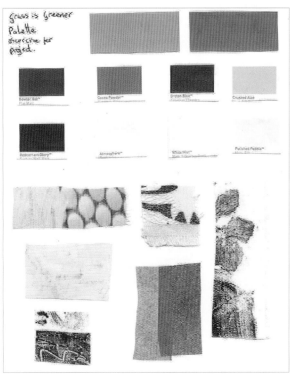

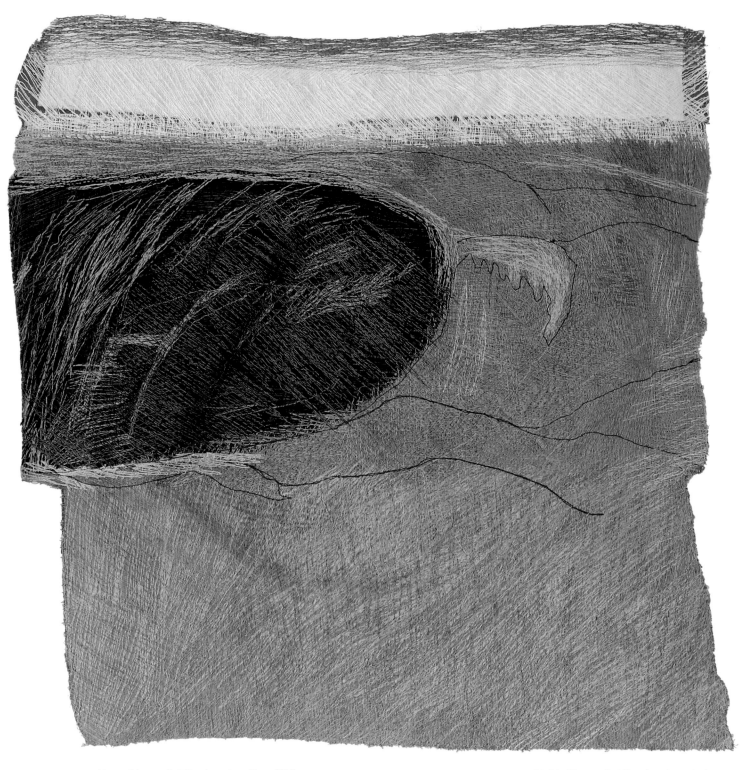

Above Dionne Swift, *Looming Sky*, 2012.
Free-machine embroidery with wool, silk,
cotton and viscose, 70 x 70 x 5cm (27½ x
27½ x 2in).

Right Dionne Swift, drawing study
for *Looming Sky*. Oil and graphite,
30 x 30cm (12 x 12in).

Dionne Swift

Artist Dionne Swift described the connection between drawing and sewing in relation to the inspiration she takes from walking in her beloved Yorkshire landscape. Her connection to the outside world is tangible and energizes the marks she makes. She relates to the rhythm that she finds in the activities, referring to the process and body of work as 'Walk, Draw, Sew', revealing:

As I WALK it takes time to loosen up, to forget my worries and woes, to get to the right speed, to find my stride, to sense the right terrain, but over time I settle into a good pace and my shoulders fall back, neck extends and hips roll and rotate as I march, building up speed, and race through the landscape. I can walk with ease whilst taking in my surroundings, observing new vistas and contemplating my movements through the land. There is not a switch to flick that makes me DRAW. I need to ease into it (much like the walking); the atmosphere and my temperament must be right – not too comfortable, though... my drawings need energy: energy that is often driven from within. I can liken the walking motion to that of sewing – I need time to settle into my machine especially if I've been away from the studio for a while; we find our rhythm and I try and remember to sit tall and straight. Before I know it, we're flying. The connection and empathy I have with my machine means that when I SEW, I sew with power and passion, with the compounded energy from my drawings. I am making marks with thread and am lost in the activity.

Above Kate Boucher drawing the shadows of a plant.

Shadow drawings

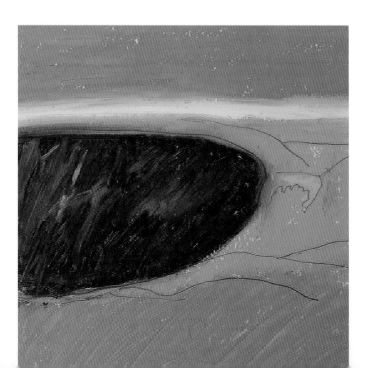

I encourage students to take a step outside the workspace to make shadow drawings, recording the outlines traced from the shadows of interesting objects, plants, or shapes of man-made architecture such as wire fencing. To do this, you need a bright, sunny day, basic drawing materials, a sketchbook or paper, and something to hold pages down in a breeze (masking tape, bulldog clips or rubber bands).

Place the paper where the shadows fall across it. (However, if you cannot get down to the shadows, bring shadows closer to you: arrange pot plants or small items on a table, and use the shadows they cast.) Start with a continuous line drawing and extend the drawing across the pages as you go. As you work, overlay one drawing on top of another using different drawing media and/or change the orientation of the sketchbook. Use different tones or even colours to represent the depth and slight colour shifts in the shadows. Textural marks and lines almost 'self-generate', as you become so absorbed in the activity that you forget that you are drawing.

Small collages: the joy of the accidental

Sometimes it is useful to work without a clear idea of what you intend to create and to explore the possibilities of a random collection of materials put aside specifically for experiments. It allows you discover processes by chance and develop your ideas, immersing yourself in aspects of colour, surface, texture and design as you work. Collage is a technique with an immediate hands-on, tactile quality familiar to the textile artist, and it can be a useful means of creating small design samples from all kinds of collected materials. Paper, magazines and cloth, including painted and stained offcuts from ongoing projects, can be saved for this purpose.

Create quick, 'random' collages by attaching the pieces you have collected to paper or a cloth base. An old postcard will do. Try to make one or two of these small pieces each day over several days; save the best ones to work with further or to take into stitch and discard the rest.

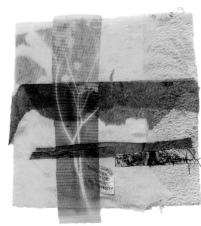

This page Green collage samples based on new growth. Collages using the same range of materials based around the theme of 'Grass is Greener'. The top two collages (right) have been held with a little glue prior to stitching. The bottom two are held with additional stitch.

You will need

- A small pile of scrap fabric/paper/ found materials
- An object or subject for inspiration: a piece of music, poetry, a single word, an old photo or one of your sketches
- Watercolour paper, card or cloth as a base
- Glue and scissors

Choose a subject to explore, or a technique that interests you. It could be something as simple as a small collection of stones, shells collected on a trip, or working to a colour theme inspired by places you have visited. Explore as many ways as you can to express that idea by creating small, collaged compositions made with textured, painted papers, coloured photocopies, drawings and text. Working in a series can expand your vision and allows you to explore themes to a greater depth. Try the following ideas:

- Create several pieces, using a combination of different techniques such as printing, drawing or stitching in each one.
- Explore different formats for the collage, though using the same materials – for example square, oblong, circular or triangular shapes. Changes in format and composition may well provide ideas for a series of modular pieces at a later stage.
- Alter a few elements of the composition at a time, to give you a series that subtly changes as it goes on, perhaps becoming more abstract.
- Try limiting colour usage: for example keep to black and white, earth tones or all greens.

Making collages in this way may seem random, but as you work, make notes and assess what is working or not working. Which themes, colour choices or forms are emerging? Start making decisions about the next stage in the process. I often refer to this process as 'backward design', as it allows you to reflect and make decisions about the work as it progresses but still be open to change.

Below *Norfolk or the Netherlands* sketchbook page. The pieces for these collages were cut out of isolations of a larger sample to create a more flowing design. This is an example of 'backward design' - extracting compositions from larger collages.

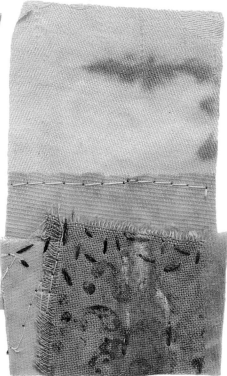

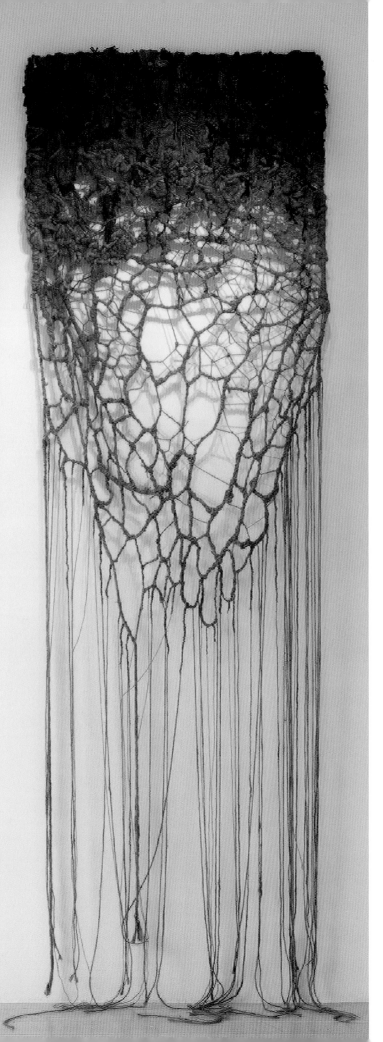

'Things': working with others

The items we turn to for inspiration need not be the things we find precious or of great beauty (as my father's old paint cards illustrate). Textile students from the Kanus faculty of the Vilnius Academy of Arts, Lithuania, worked in collaboration with students from the textiles department of the CIT Crawford College of Art and Design, Cork, to develop pieces in response to the 'things' of the everyday. The artist Pamela Hardesty, who led the project, described its rationale:

Our world is increasingly a fabric of unregarded things: the functional, everyday, and ordinary objects of our lives. Usually factory-made, often global in their reach, seemingly identity-less, these things have become, in this project, the deeply considered clues to culture and meaning.

(PAMELA HARDESTY, 2014)

Each student selected an ordinary item from their observations of daily life (these included buttons, till rolls, keys, wire, milk-bottle tops and hair clips) and then wrote down as many words and phrases as possible associated with their 'thing'. From these lists, two words were selected as a key from which the identities of the objects would be drawn out, discussed, documented and formed into textile samples for exchange online and sending through the post to the partnering college. Through research and exchange, the students in each country gained insight into the associated meanings of each object and also the culture of each country.

Ann Mechelinck

The central theme in Ann Mechelinck's knotted work is of letting go. Her starting point for the piece was a key and the words 'possession' and 'freedom'. Knotted and dyed strips of fabric, upholstery tassels and jute rope are supported on a metal frame. She discusses the pieces as representing people feeling lost, imprisoned and pressured by thoughts of 'must have', 'must do' and 'need to', and the everyday concerns surrounding materialism and our obligations and expectations. She talks of translating these feelings in the construction of the knots 'that need to be untied and untangled if we want to find that freedom and harmony to grow again'.

Left Ann Mechelinck, fabrics, upholstery tassels and jute rope, 96 x 197cm (37¾ x 77½in).

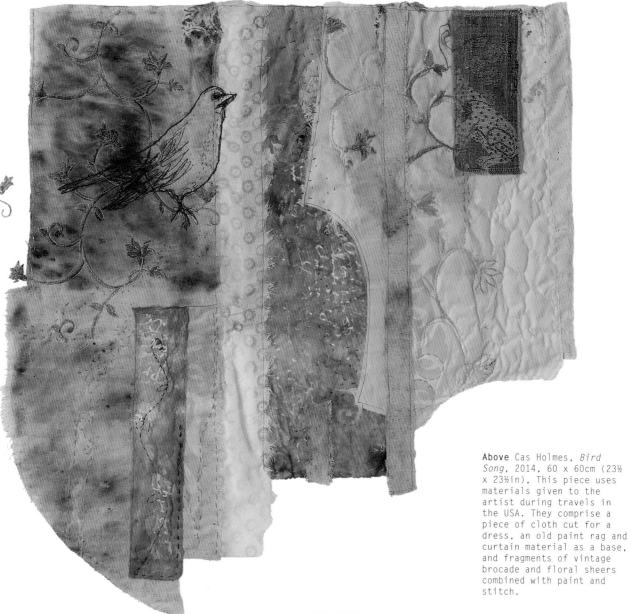

Above Cas Holmes, *Bird Song*, 2014, 60 x 60cm (23½ x 23½in). This piece uses materials given to the artist during travels in the USA. They comprise a piece of cloth cut for a dress, an old paint rag and curtain material as a base, and fragments of vintage brocade and floral sheers combined with paint and stitch.

Margarita Žigutytė

Margarita Žigutytė is interested in how things change over time and the idea of the temporary. She questions consumer culture, which forgets traditions and values. In *Priceless Object* she referenced traditional Lithuanian belt patterns and printed the design on to receipt-roll paper, which changes when heated, explaining: 'Heated paper changes its colour, but after some time patterns are starting to disappear, like our past and memories. And yet, there will always be things that will always stay with our humanity – crafts and textile.'

Right Margarita Žigutyte, *Priceless Object* (2014). Originally presented as a long strip of till roll, this grid of patterned details shows the interaction between the stitched mark and the disappearing marks of the heat-transferred image on the till roll.

Our response to cloth

Cloth, in its intimate relationship with our body, bears the marks of our being, both on the surface and embedded within the structure. The strains, stresses, stains and smells we impress upon this second skin form an archive of our most intimate life. At the same time, cloth is also the membrane through which we establish our sense of 'becoming', and formalize our relationship with the external world, while the fabric remorselessly records the evidence of those interactions. Cloth holds the memory of our time and connects us with memories of other times and other places.

(LESLEY MILLAR, 2012)

Above, inset Cloth samples with frayed and distressed edges. These include a vintage Edinburgh landscape sample showing both the front and back of the stitch and samples of Japanese and French woven cloth.

Above Jeanette Appleton, *Production Line*, 2013. Felted books on location at Salts Mill, Saltaire.

Lesley Millar, curator of the 'Cloth & Memory' exhibitions that took place at Salts Mill, Saltaire, Yorkshire in 2012 and 2013, argues that it is the specific qualities we find in cloth that make it a suitable medium for the expression of our ideas and the representation of memory. Our response to cloth is individual, yet conversely there is a shared or 'common' association: textiles have a relationship with the people who made them, with a given time when they were used or worn, and with the places they come from. We all treasure pieces that hold special memories associated with family or friends. We could argue that cloth, paper and fibre come with a narrative or 'memory' – physical, functional and emotional – and this consideration informs the design process.

Let's look at the narrative aspects of cloth that we might examine for a project.

Looking at cloth

• What are the physical properties of the cloth and what is it made from?
• What is its handle? Is it stiff, soft or starched?
• What is its construction? Is it woven, non-woven, knitted, lacy, felted, bonded or natural?
• Has it been dyed or printed? Which treatments has the cloth undergone?
• Is it transparent? Does it have a pile, nap or direction? What is its texture? What weight of cloth is it?
• Is it a non-traditional or synthetic cloth? Is it a new material, such as Tyvek, which can be used for protective clothing?
• What is or was its function or history of use?

- Was it functional or ornamental?
- Was it for domestic or personal items?
- Is it worn or as new?
- Was it used for ceremonial, ritual or celebratory purposes?
- Does it bear the imprint of wear and tear – stains, tears, patches or darns?
- Is it historical clothing, no longer in use now?
- Was it used for protection, overalls or a uniform?
- What emotional response does it evoke? What are our individual memories of, or connections to, the cloth?
- Are the colours evocative of a time and place, such as summer prints, or autumnal wools?
- Does it make us nostalgic? Does it have associations with childhood, family, happy times or loss?
- Does it have a connection to a place or environment? Or to a recycling ethos?
- Are there any cultural, social, psychological or religious connections?
- What are your physical responses to the smell of the cloth? Does it engender feelings of warmth and comfort when you touch it?

Below Yoriko Yoneyama, *Rice Dreams*, 2013. Shown on location at Salts Mill, Saltaire.

'Cloth & Memory 2'

For the exhibition 'Cloth & Memory 2', 23 international artists were invited to draw upon their associations with 'cloth' and propose new, site-specific works in response to the vast spinning room at the former textile mill (Salts Mill is a UNESCO World Heritage Site). The mill has not been restored or refurbished, aside from a new roof, and the internal architecture, with its peeling walls and floors, still retains the marks and smells of its original use.

Jeanette Appleton related cloth to the noise of the busy lives of people working in the mill and used the 'silencing' context of felt as a metaphor for the absorption of sound and memory. Intimate works based on the original ledgers and sample books were placed in the wall cavities once used by workers to store bobbins. This partial concealment in the cavity required the viewer to move around, crouch down, move forward or back in response to the work.

Yoriko Yoneyama was interested in the overlooked elements which are essential to our survival and our cultural heritage: food and clothing; rice and fibre. Her installation at Salts Mill was made up of dried rice painstakingly threaded on to fine cotton suspended from the beams and reflected in free-standing and floor-based mirrors.

From drawing to cloth

Approaches to the translation of a drawing to cloth vary from maker to maker. Marks can be made with dry media, paint, dye and, of course, in stitch. Here are some things to try:

• Draw your design on the reverse of the fabric and stitch through to the front.

• Make a drawing on tissue or a lightweight sheer material and stitch it down on the free-machine setting on a sewing machine or by hand. You can tear the tissue away afterwards. If using sheer material, cut it away carefully or leave it in place before adding another layer.

• Paint or draw directly on the cloth with fabric paints or dilute acrylic paint. Further detail can be added with stitch. The painting of cloth can provide interesting background surfaces for interaction with stitch.

• Photographically transfer your image to the cloth's surface. (This is covered in more detail on pages 88–89.)

• Machine stitch or hand stitch freely directly on to the cloth. This is my usual method, with the sketchbook beside me. I feel this allows for greater fluidity in the marks I make with the machine or by hand.

From left to right Small stitched collages.

Above right *Bird Song* (detail). This detail shows the machine-stitched bird against the painted cloth background (an old paint rag). The ends of the machine threads have been stitched back into the machine stitching to add textural detail (see page 35 for the complete piece).

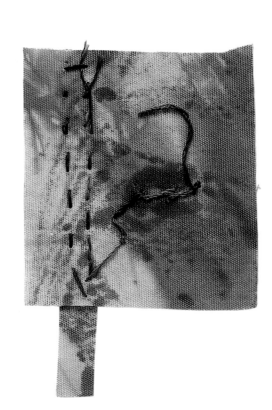

Creating a space for inspiration

Hard work isn't always productive. Sometimes you need to switch off, go for walk, listen to music, do something else or even do nothing. Your brain needs to have an away day at times. These are my top tips for creating space for inspiration:

• Collaborate. Spend time with someone else: I am inspired by conversations and exchanges of ideas, which help me to see the world differently and challenge my usual view of things. It is just as possible to be inspired by a writer, gardener, musician or friend as by a visual artist.

• Observe and seek out stories. I am inspired by stories of place and observe my surroundings acutely. Investigate, ask questions, and find out interesting details and stories.

• Be open to your surroundings and explore the character of places or situations. Find inspiration in the minutiae of daily life (food packaging, travel tickets and street signs, for example). When travelling in unfamiliar territory, investigate everyday things anew.

• Daydream: journeys on public transport are a good opportunity to daydream.

• Always have something to write or draw on. You never know when a good idea might creep up on you.

• Have a hobby or something else to do other than make art. I seem to think about art all the time, but I like reading and watching films, or going for a walk, as ways to switch off from this. However, sometimes these other pursuits generate memories of things I have seen or read a long time ago and act as a source of inspiration or build up connections in my work.

• Destroy and let go of things. Don't be afraid to abandon all your planning and hard work and explore a different approach at the last minute. It's hard to let go, but sometimes you need to start afresh to explore new possibilities in your work.

• It is okay to make mistakes and make a mess, but review your workspace and periodically tidy it up.

• Work doesn't always have to make sense!

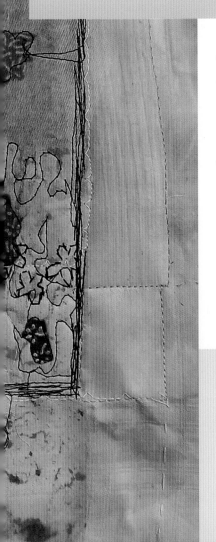

THE NATURAL WORLD

The world we live in provides an abundance of natural resources to draw upon for inspiration. It has long been a source of reference for the artist and this is no less relevant for those of us who chose to work in cloth and stitch. The natural world provides physical resources such as plants and gathered materials for the artist to work with, as well as visual stimulation for our ideas. These ideas are drawn from the ever-changing landscape and the more intimate detritus and colours of our urban spaces and gardens. This chapter looks at different approaches to recording the landscapes valued by various artists.

Common places: a natural resource

The slow slippage in one's visual grasp of the environment has other origins in the Yare Valley, particularly in autumn and winter, when the waves of sun-warmed air radiating back off the land hit the cold blast of night, to condense as a fine veil above the horizon. This mist first congeals over the water-filled dykes and then spills in linear shoals out across the fields, gradually back-filling the landscape, winding through the trees, submerging the fixed properties of day in a soft white nebula. Sometimes it lies upon everything in a perfect sheet or encircles the trees, deepening steadily until their tops rise like a free-floating island of vegetation.

(MARK COCKER, 2007)

In a description of Norfolk, Mark Cocker (2007) refers to a landscape where 'commonplace items are blurred and assume unfamiliar characteristics'. The natural world provides an infinitely rich and ever-changing resource for artists, displaying new sources of inspiration at different times of day, in a range of weathers, which are revealed with each season. Whether you are stimulated by open expanses of countryside, local parks or urban back gardens, there is always something fresh to explore.

Above *Rushes* book form, 2013, 42 x 12 x 12cm (16½x 5 x 5in). The stitched drawing on a piece of packaging found on location has been used to create the blurred print on this folded textile piece, evoking the watery field of the landcape.

Connecting
materials to places

A visual artist makes connections to place and time as effectively as a writer or a musician: we just use a different set of creative tools. The artist Andy Goldsworthy, reflecting on his creative process in 1990, stated: 'I stop at a place or pick up material because I feel that there is something to be discovered. Here is where I can learn.' He discusses material as having a distinct connection to a place in time as part of his process of discovery.

Arguably, my artwork could be made with any material, but cloth and paper have a familiarity of purpose that I enjoy and utilize. The surfaces of old fabrics and paper worn with age are a testimony to their specific functions, from the cloth used for apparel and to provide warmth, comfort and colour in the home to paper used for writing or for the wrapping of parcels. When deciding on materials to work with, consider the following:

• Is the relationship that a material has to a given place relevant to the portrayal of your ideas? For example, materials collected from a family holiday, or a visit to a museum or gallery. When I salvaged cleaning rags from the repainting of a lightship (see page 110–111), these became a main source of inspiration, connecting the material in a piece of work to the ship where it was found.

• Which naturally growing resources can we use for textile work? We have long used dyes, and made baskets, bags and clothing from plant materials. Is the feel of a naturally growing fibre or the habitat of a plant relevant to the construction of the piece?

• Furnishings, interior decorating fabrics and their references to natural and geometric forms connect interior and exterior spaces and can also serve as a reminder of a specific time or a place. The bright psychedelic flowers I had on my bedroom walls in the late 1960s tie me to memories of listening to *Top of the Pops* on the radio and images of pop art.

• Finally, unusual synthetics salvaged from environmental waste, industrial fabrics or new organic materials can suggest a different way of working with 'cloth'. Sailcloth, roofing Tyvek or garden fleece can be used to create large installations. Look at how theatre designers or window dressers use fabrics on a large scale.

Above Rachel Doolin, *Deconstructing Demeter*, Milk-protein fibre and dandelion seeds, 116 x 54 x 122cm (45½ x 21¼ x 48in). Work produced in response to the project brief for 'Things/Daiktai' and resulting exhibition at CIT Wandesford Quay Gallery, Cork, 2014 (see page 110-111).

Rachel Doolin

In *Deconstructing Demeter* (above), a work produced for the 'Things/ Daiktai' project and exhibition at CIT Wandesford Quay Gallery, Cork, in 2014, Rachel Doolin created a fabric from milk-protein fibre and dandelion seeds. She is concerned with the scientific advances that allow genetic engineering and the modification of species that are evident in the cycles of cultivation, production and consumption. The seeds have become symbolic objects – she states: 'Human interference has rendered the seeds sterile, thus creating a field of impossible dreams.' She further discusses the work as emulating 'a false cultivation production process in which the utilitarian application of science and technology has given us the power to manipulate and control natural processes for the advancement of humankind'.

From the land: sustainable stitch

The biodiversity of our landscape is constantly being eroded by our demands upon the land and arguments about land use are echoed in the reports by wildlife conservation organizations. In their report *England's Green Unpleasant Land?*, the organization Plant Life describes the loss of much the national habitat of our ancient grasslands as follows:

Unimproved grassland is now mostly found in small fragments, and it is threatened by this fragmentation. The scraps can be found in small fields isolated from each other – pieces of wildflower-rich road verge, village greens, scraps of downland too steep to plough, churchyards, rides and glades within ancient woods and patches of acid grassland on commons.

(MILES KING 2002)

The report argues that changes in land use, building practice and advances in farming are at the heart of the problem, and a more sustainable approach is required. I like to take a parallel approach in my textile work and to reuse materials wherever possible. It is an ethical – as well as a creative – choice that is becoming more widely practised by artists. The instructions sent to students attending one of my courses usually include a materials list requesting that they bring a small bag filled with discarded cloth, paper and found items as a resource to use. This practice is reflected in my home, which is furnished and decorated with items discovered in charity shops, skips, salvage yards and donated by friends – all to be 'upcycled' and re-created.

Looking at our relationship with the world around us – the colours, patterns and shapes we see – can be a very broad resource for inspiration and materials. In a small, crowded country such as the UK, people and nature need to co-exist. The small tracts of land we leave wild in our urban spaces, verges at the side of the road, or the edges of fields are important environmental route ways for flora and fauna, and can be useful to us, too. My grandmother would have collected berries from the roadsides in the autumn and made use of other plants, willow and herbs she found. I too find myself picking plants for drawing and printing, as well as discarded items in the streets, old labels, string and many other things we readily throw away, as I forage for materials for my own work. Working 'on the move' like this allows for a greater interplay between your work and the world around you.

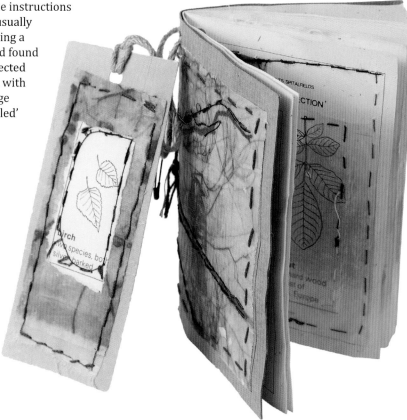

Right *Tree-Book*, 2012. This book was made from a label found in local woods. The whole label was a book-like instruction for 'care'. Obviously, that 'care' did not extend to the woodland.

Above *Bluebell*, 2011, 105 x 105cm (41 x 41in).
Represented in the Embroiderer's Guild collection.
The quilt uses hand-dyed cloth and paper
incorporating fabrics gathered from my family home
and transfers of my father's handwritten text.

Mixed-media backgrounds for stitch

I like to create layered mixed-media backgrounds for stitching into. The remnants of domestic life, washed rags and cloth marked with paint or stains, worn layers of old fabrics, tea towels, tablecloths, handkerchiefs and clothing evidencing 'human contact' are my materials of choice for backgrounds. I work intuitively, and the rituals of making, layering cloth and paper mark the passing of time and act as part of the narrative of the work.

The connection between printing, painting and drawing, and the slower act of stitching, gives unexpected results. The interaction of colour, texture and pattern when working in response to the materials produces surfaces that can be full of depth, subtlety and movement. As I work, I cut, tear and stitch back into the papers and fabrics, excavating colour and shapes from the layers of cloth and paint. The process could be described as 'design by destruction'; the size, format and colours of each piece constantly change and the composition is only realized on completion. The basic process for making

layered pieces using cellulose paste is a form of 'wet appliqué' which, when dry, creates a newly constructed 'cloth' that provides a stable foundation for machine stitching. (You can find more detail on this process in my book *The Found Object in Textile Art*.)

In preparation for making a mixed-media background, I usually look through my collection of 'found stuff'. I gather a range of textiles and papers in colours and surfaces I think are suitable for creating the foundation or base for a stitched piece (porous and natural materials such as pre-washed cotton, linens, handmade papers, lightweight tissues or paper napkins). I often use a fine conservation or archival interleaving tissue or Tissuetex (see Glossary, page 123) in this process in some of the top layers to hold small pieces and fragments in place. When doing this yourself, as you build and overlay the torn and cut pieces, refer to drawings and studies in your sketchbook, or look at your photographic images, to help with structure and composition.

Left *Iris Canvas*, 2013, both 20 x 20cm (8 x 8in). The iris was directly printed on to handmade paper by pressing it in a bookbinding press overnight. The colours of the iris leached on to the paper. The paper was stitched and then applied to a small canvas with thickened wallpaper paste.

Opposite, top *The Grass is Greener*, 2012, 40 x 40cm (16 x 16in). One from a series of four panels using a set of linen napkins (donated by one of my students) as a base. Transfer prints of wild flowers and stitched drawings reflect conservation work on the royal estates of Sandringham and Windsor. It is a comment on the lesser-known story of the environmental and land-management work of the royal family.

Opposite, centre Laying out the collages on a napkin base, working on all four at the same time. Similar materials have been used in all the compositions.

Far opposite, below Detail from *The Grass is Greener*, showing the tea towel in the centre with stitched and dyed cloth either side.

to separate and remove pieces, or add other elements to the composition before starting to stitch. Where you have used mostly textile-based materials, the paste can also be washed out after stitching; however, leaving the paste in the work presents no problem, as it will soften as you handle the piece when working on it.

5 You can apply paints and dyes to materials in order to change their colour and texture. Remember that these may also alter absorption of the paste – for example, a thick acrylic paint medium will resist the paste.

6 If you do not intend to stitch the surface, or when working on top of a canvas, stronger adhesion methods (such as PVA glue or an acrylic gel medium) will be needed for a more permanent fix. Alternatively, use an iron-on interfacing such as Bondaweb. This bonds with the fabric permanently, so it is less easy to adjust the cloth or paper when fixed into place.

The wet-appliqué process

You will need

- Cellulose wallpaper paste or cellulose paste powder (also known as methyl cellulose). Wallpaper paste may contain fungicide
- Plastic sheeting
- A broad soft brush about 2-3cm (1in) wide
- Plastic container for the paste
- Collection of medium to lightweight fabrics and papers

1 Mix up the paste to about a half to a third of its recommended strength. You will need to experiment with its consistency as atmospheric conditions (heat and moisture), together with the absorbency and weight of the materials you are layering, will affect drying time and adhesion.

2 Using plastic sheeting as a work surface, set down large pieces of fabric and/or paper as a foundation. Paste thoroughly with a brush, ensuring that the paste works its way through all the layers. Add smaller pieces on top of the larger pieces of fabric, again holding them down with paste. When dry, the paste will have lightly held the layered fabrics and papers together into a loose collage of cloth and materials. Remove this new 'cloth' from the plastic backing.

3 The resulting cloth surface can be machine-stitched to both hold and change the shape or feel of the material. Free-motion stitching using a darning foot will create loose, free-flowing lines. I often refer to the marks I make with my pen or pencil in a sketchbook as a means to inform the texture and form of my stitching.

4 Observe and experiment with the way that the layers adhere to each other. The paste is only a temporary fix that is intended to be reversible. Some of the layers may loosen with handling. These can be re-pasted or pinned as you work, allowing you

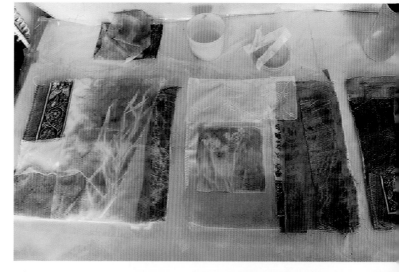

Garden and landscape inspirations

Gardens provide a wonderful resource for stimulating ideas. The medium of textiles has a long association with plants and flowers, both as a subject for art and design and as a natural dye resource. Colour will naturally leach out of plant material when it is placed under pressure and so plants can be pressed to give delicate prints. Many of our textiles, summer dresses, furnishings and even our walls are covered with designs that take their inspiration from the various plants, flowers and wildlife in gardens.

You can create your own response to a garden in a drawing, with paint or in cloth to celebrate seasonal changes, and the observations you make can be richly rewarding. If you do not have a garden, you can enjoy the gardens created by others. There are a host of gardens open to the public throughout the UK, from the internationally renowned Kew Botanical Gardens, the gardens of the Crown Estate and the National Trust to local parks that are more intimate in scale and private gardens open as part of the National Garden Scheme. If you are visiting a garden that is open to the public, early mornings or weekdays are often the best time to find a quiet spot in which to work. The most obvious attraction is the fine planting, which gives a riot of colour and different shapes and forms. But there is another aspect too: a garden is an enclosed (often quite private) space, a landscape in miniature, which makes it an approachable subject to work with.

Selecting a subject

There are, of course, difficulties inherent in such a broad subject, as there are many different aspects of a garden from which to select a theme. Try looking in detail, as if under a magnifying lens, and focus on specific plants or textures such as the patterns and shapes in foliage, shadows on a path, or the ripples and reflections in water. It will help to lead to work with textural and colour interest. Most point-and-shoot cameras have a zoom that allows you to record incredible detail, which you can build on back in the studio.

Left Collage in sketchbook of a garden corner in the shade.

The preservation of the land and the production of good, sustainable food is once again a consideration for farming communities. Small farms also need to be inventive in order to generate income. At Newhouse Farm in Cornwall, Jo and Stephen Colwill have found enterprising ways of bringing ethical farming practice, good food and a love of quilting together in their Cowslip Workshops, where they run textile courses. A small organic garden provides many of the vegetables for the café, but equally, plants are gathered for printing and dyeing. Inspiration is drawn from sketches made of the beautiful Cornish countryside and old farm buildings typical of the British landscape. The more intimate corners of a working garden, with its collection of pots, tools and plants, can provide a wonderful stimulus for developing little 'garden portraits'.

Above Ink and watercolour study of a garden corner at Cowslip Workshops in Launceton, Cornwall.

Above *Cowslip Watering Can*. Machine and hand stitch on a collage of fabrics gathered on location, 2014.

Above Cas Holmes, *Alf's Reed Warbler*, 2014. This piece was made with a handkerchief donated by Alf's granddaughter. She carried and used the handkerchief until it became threadbare. Many men who fought on the Western Front wrote letters home that reported hearing birdsong in the quiet between gunfire. Nesting birds were often 'adopted' and daily inspections organized to ensure they were safe.

Stitching the First World War

The story behind a particular garden and the collections it may hold can lead to work of social or historical significance. For example, a project organized as part of a commemorative exhibition, 'Gardens and War', to mark the centenary of the outbreak of the First World War was held at the Garden Museum in Lambeth in 2014. It testified to the value of 'historical narrative' as a creative and social activity for stitch. Working with the support of Age UK Bromley and Greenwich Community Volunteers' Time Bank (CVTB), as part of a weekly meeting, participants informally recollected individual stories over tea and biscuits in the context of gardening and memories of family.

Handling the hand-embroidered postcards and handkerchiefs of the period led to discussions about how these items acted as poignant reminders of home and of nature, helping people to cope with the hardship of war. Using a collection of found materials, participants explored a range of techniques and layered images and drawings on to fabric handkerchiefs. With each stitch, new stories and long-forgotten painting and embroidery skills were uncovered and exchanged as part of the process. Liz Kent, CVTB manager at Age UK Bromley and Greenwich, remembers:

There seemed to be no loss of continuity between sessions, with some people carrying on with their sewing at home and others meeting to sew together. It was a great project to be part of. The swapping of sewing skills mirrors the wider skill swapping that happens within the Time Bank, which was set up to tackle social isolation amongst older people.

Garden of Remembrance reflects the stories of serving men (and women) and those working on the Home Front in the newly founded Women's Land Army and the Women's Institute. It also includes a reference to Edith Cavell, the Norfolk-born nurse executed by the Germans during the war. During the war years, children and adults grew and collected medicinal plants and herbs from the wild (to compensate for the loss of German pharmaceutical products on which Britain was heavily dependent), and seeds were grown and distributed by gardeners and allotment holders for the growing of vegetables and fruit as imports dwindled.

Right *Garden of Remembrance*, commission for the Garden Museum, 2014, 80 x 120cm (31½ x 47in). Constructed from found and donated materials related to the themes of gardening, this piece is based on stories, history, personal observations and material connected to the First World War. Inspiration has come from original historical material as part of the archive of The Garden Museum (see also detail on page 5).

Connecting to nature

Noriko Endo

Noriko Endo finds inspiration in the landscape and gardens of her native Japan. Using photographs taken on regular walks or from her travels, she makes 'confetti quilts' from very small pieces of fabric, creating the appearance of an impressionist painting. Noriko's husband often helps with the painting and preparation of the fabric, and each quilt takes several months to complete. In *Cherry Blossom*, her husband hand-painted the centre of each blossom.

Noriko cuts coloured fabric into tiny pieces quickly and fluidly with a rotary cutter or scissors. These are then organized into tidy groups of colours and stored ready for use on her projects.

Noriko uses wadding (laid on top of the base fabric) as a 'canvas' and with a painter's eye, places coloured bits of fabric directly on top of it as if laying down a broad brush of background colour, prior to adding detail. She covers this with fine tulle and then adds more definition with further fabric and layers of tulle. Tree trunks or regular shapes are often inserted as shapes carefully cut from hand-dyed fabric. All the layers of tulle are pinned into place, finishing with a last layer of fine black tulle pinned every 5cm (2in.).

The built-up layers are then free-machine-stitched with a long-arm quilting machine using a monofilament thread which is more or less invisible. When everything is anchored, Noriko applies textural detail using the free-machine setting on a standard sewing machine. For smaller pieces, it is possible to use a standard machine for the entire process.

Above Noriko Endo. *Cherry Blossom #3*. 2004. Cotton, tulle, silk, luminescent fibres, polyester wadding, cotton backing and paint. Techniques include machine appliqué, quilting and embellishment. 220 x 168cm (87 x 66in).

Above Cherry blossom is one of Japan's symbolic flowers.

Above Shadow transfer photo of plants. The plants are placed fresh between the paper, which has been painted with transfer paint, and the cloth as it is ironed to leave the negative image of the plants.

Have nothing in your house that you do not know to be useful, or believe to be beautiful.

William Morris

Designs that reference the natural world have a long legacy. The famous designs of William Morris and the Arts & Crafts Movement are still available and can be seen in textiles and wallpaper today. Morris was a leading figure in the movement, and felt that the 'diligent study of Nature' was important to the artist as nature was the perfect example of 'God's design' and the 'spiritual antidote' to what to he perceived as the decline in social, moral and artistic standards during the Industrial Revolution. This spiritual antidote is equally relevant to counter the fast-paced, information-packed, technology-based lifestyle we have today. Fabrics and ceramics featuring designs from nature help bring the outside environment into the interior space.

Winter strategies

As we enter winter, we start to miss the richness of the outdoors. The trees begin to lose their leaves and it can feel as if the world becomes a little smaller and emptier as we withdraw to the warmth of our indoor spaces. Yet windows allow the shadows and patterns from our gardens and trees to ripple and move on furniture and walls. My drawings and observations now begin to focus on the small objects, bowls, boxes and fabrics brought back from travels in Japan, Hong Kong and India; also finds discovered when out walking locally, such as shells, seedpods and animal bones. Everyday household items, the view from a window, and your own collection of found objects can provide a wealth of interest and make useful starting points for new projects during the winter months.

Above *Red Bowl*, 44 x 44cm, 2012. Napkin base, transfer, oriental paper, machine and hand stitch. The drawings for the bowl were made at a time when I was restricted to my bed through illness and could not walk.

The true secret of happiness lies in taking a genuine interest in all the details of daily life.

WILLIAM MORRIS

Tracing shadows: heat-transfer printing

My usage of dyes and paint media on cloth and paper is informed by the marks I make on paper or in sketchbooks, but the materials behave and respond in different ways. Cloth varies in its absorbency and take-up of colour, acrylic paint can be diluted and used as a wash, and ink from pens will bleed and follow the weave of the fabric. The methods I use often reflect the season and practicalities of working with found materials that are available at the time. In the summer, on the rare hot days we have, I work outside to dye some of my stash of fabrics, where they bleed and bleach as they dry in the sun. I also collect and use plant material for sun-printing and eco dyeing (see Holly Story, pages 61–63). In the shorter, long-shadowed days of late autumn through to early spring, I am drawn to the shapes and shadows that connect the interior and outside space. I paint and mark finely printed fabrics and discarded nets with transfer (disperse) dyes, or fabric crayons, or I simply stain them to reflect the changing patterns of the season. This process is also less demanding on space and drying areas when I am also fighting to get the laundry done in my small house!

Transfer dyeing

Transfer or disperse dyeing is the process of painting dyes on to paper and then using that painted paper to transfer the colour to fabric with a hot iron or press. Wax-transfer fabric crayons work in a similar way. These specialist disperse dyes were created in the 1920s to colour the new synthetic fabrics such as nylon.

You can work on synthetic fabrics such as polyester and nylon, and wool blends and cotton blends that have a synthetic fibre content of more than 60 per cent (these will achieve a softer colour). When painted on paper, the dye colours may initially appear dull; full colour will only appear once they have been activated by heat. It is worth sampling and testing the papers you intend to colour with the transfer paint, as well as the materials you intend to print on to, in advance. This will also give you an opportunity to check the iron setting and transfer time, and the resulting colours.

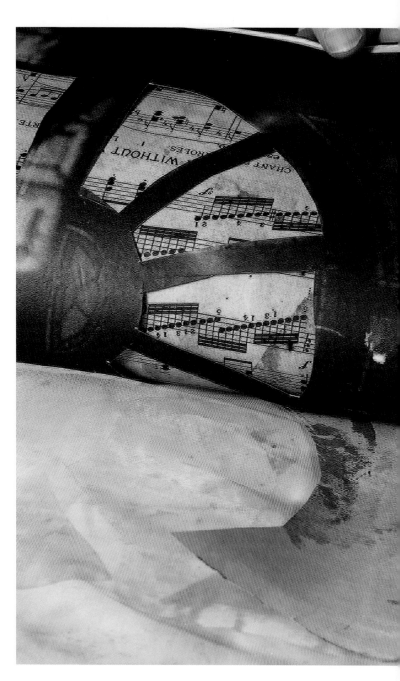

Above Transfer in progress for *Waterland* textile collage. The transfer papers were cut into shapes to create the window motif.

Quantities

You can mix up your own disperse/transfer solution from powder or buy the dye ready mixed. To make transfer paint from powdered dye to a thin consistency, measure out 10–100g of dye (depending on the depth of colour required) and sprinkle it into 500ml of tepid water. Stir vigorously and leave to stand for five minutes

Printing with transfer paints

1 Brush, paint, stencil or spray the transfer paint on to smooth paper and allow it to dry. Photocopier paper and clean (unprinted) newsprint work equally well. Remember that the design will be reversed when you print it. I like to work with printed photocopy paper; this will often leave a subtle image of the print as part of the transfer.

2 Cover your ironing board with an old cloth to protect it and use as an underlay. Cover with several layers of clean newsprint or paper. Lay the fabric on top. Place the design on top of the fabric, paint-side down. Place a piece of greaseproof paper between the iron and the back of the design to protect the iron. Set the iron's thermostat to a temperature somewhere between that specified for wool and cotton (use the setting for cotton if the fabric is a natural fibre/synthetic mix) and iron for one to two minutes. For small papers, keep the iron still, since movement can blur the image. The transfer will be complete when the paper begins to yellow.

- For larger patterns, it is advisable to set one area at a time, with a cooling time between each. I apply firm pressure with the iron whilst slowly moving it over the paper. I keep my hand on the iron and take a peek by lifting the edge of the paper carefully to see if the image has transferred.

- Transfers can be used more than once to make multiple prints, but each subsequent application will give a duller image with some colour change. The dye colours are intermixable, non-toxic, water-based and wash-fast.

NB. You can also use a heat press for this process but will need to test temperature and length of times for pressing in relation to the materials being used.

Notes on transfer printing

When using any dye, print or paint method, look at different approaches you can take to vary the marks and colours you make with the media. Explore a range of papers, cutting and shaping them before ironing the transfer paint on to the fabric, to create overlays with greater depth.

1 Consider the following approaches when applying paints or crayons to the paper:
- Mask areas of the paper with stencils before applying the paint.
- Rub textured surfaces with fabric crayons.
- Fold, crumple or pleat paper before dyeing or drawing on it with fabric crayons.
- Draw on paper after staining it with transfer dye.
- Apply transfer dyes to pre-cut paper such as doilies or luggage labels.

2 When ironing the paper to transfer the dye, here are some things to try:
- Iron on to plain, printed or dyed fabric.
- Tear or cut the papers into shapes before ironing.
- Layer one transfer on top of another.
- Place a cut shape, a paper doily or some lace between the transfer paper and the cloth.
- Lay patterned net curtains over the cloth before making the transfer.

3 Experimenting with cutting and layering the transfers can create unexpected effects. A student on one of my courses made the following observation of the process:

It is very hard to cut into a beautiful print or even a photocopied image on paper just in case once cut, it seems wrong. I guess the trick is to have confidence in your ability to make choices and if you make the wrong choice this time, learn from it. Cut pieces that may not work in this composition could work in another, so keep hold of them!

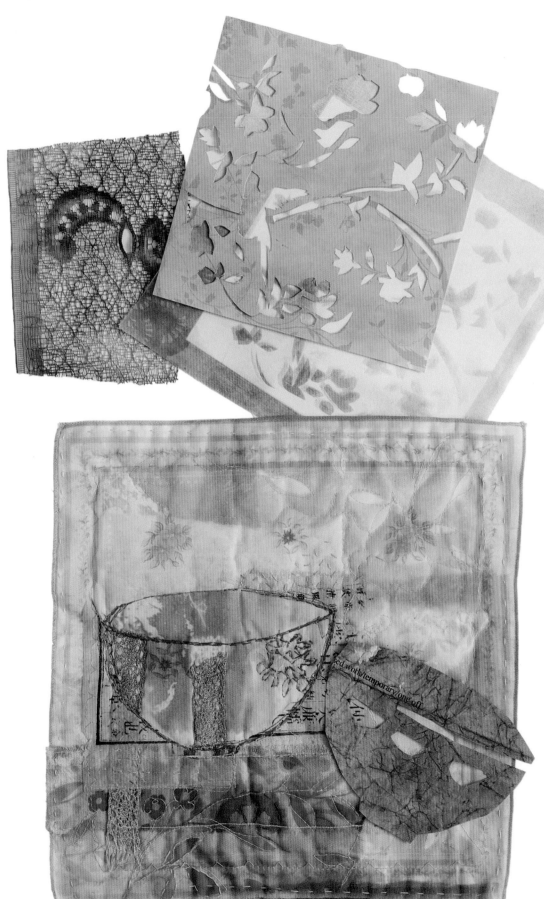

Left Cups and bowls transfer on handkerchief.The lace and wallpaper-cut stencils were used in the construction of the transfer as a resist between the cloth and the transfer paper.

Far left *Waterland*, from the series *40 Yards*, 2013, 60 x 61cm (23½ x 24in). Note the floral motifs and window stencils which were applied as transfers to this mixed-media piece before being worked in machine and hand stitch.

From the land: textures and time

I walk or cycle to and from places of work; longer journeys require me to hop on a train or bus. It is a good opportunity to observe the changing light at dawn and dusk, and this draws me to memories of my native Norfolk. In autumn, the edges of commonplace things such as trees, buildings and fields become softened by the encroaching dark, with long shadows crossing the landscape. Morning mists and sharp frosts blur outlines and make the landscape less familiar.

In spring, bright sun in the early morning or at the end of the day brings out textural details. Shapes and form become more apparent: for example furrows in the earth catch the slanting rays of the sun, or a row of trees, tall grasses and the lines of fences on the edges of a field appear as if etched on a hazy background. These details, shapes and textures from the landscape provide stimulating references for making your own narrative marks in cloth, paper and stitch. Capture such textures in photographs, or in a simple textural drawing.

Above Series of photographic studies based on the different seasons in the Norfolk landscape demonstrating both textures and the shapes of the plants and the earth.

Left *Shorelines*, 2010. There are six panels in total, each 160 x 40cm (63 x 16in). Incorporates images of photographs taken on location, monoprint, layered paper and textiles, machine and hand stitch.

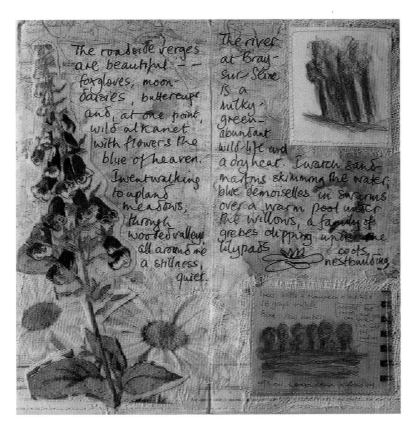

Left Ann Somerset Miles, *Nature Trail*, Journal, image of foxglove bonded to map base, scanned and stitched sketchbook pages.

Below Ann Somerset Miles, *Iris*. Iris altered through Photoshop, layout paper, bonded to background and stitched.

Ann Somerset Miles

Artist and writer Ann Somerset Miles (whose journal-making process is mentioned on page 14) uses paper napkins, maps, found papers, fabrics and re-purposed photographic images in narrative journals that reflect her interest in the garden, seasonal changes in the landscape, and her travels.

She uses a variety of methods in her fabric and paper journals, all involving various permutations of the following materials: calico, muslin and cheesecloth; three-ply paper napkins; Daler-Rowney 45 gsm layout paper; iron-on fusible webbing (Bondaweb); Golden matte gel medium; Art Van Go acrylic wax; and printed photographic images.

In her work *Nature Trail*, illustrated above, Ann wanted the foxglove to dominate and stand proud of the altered map page. She recalls:

I took one complete napkin and separated the three layers. The top layer of the napkin containing the image was fused to Bondaweb and then to calico. [For this process,] ensure that baking parchment is placed above and below the sandwich to prevent any material that is being fused sticking to the iron. Finally, apply fusible Bondaweb to the calico side of the sandwich and when cool, you can easily cut around the motif and the Bondaweb is already attached for fusing to your journal page or artwork.

Ann regularly uses cheesecloth scraps to bring together disparate components in a journal and also scans her on-the-spot journal pages to use in her work (the image can then be manipulated in Photoshop and altered in size to fit in the design of the piece before printing on layout paper). The printed layout paper is then pasted with a small amount of matte gel medium, applied with a brush or sponge (as an

alternative to fusible webbing), and pressed firmly into place on a scrap of cheesecloth or fine fabric. When stitched, it has the appearance and feel of fabric.

Ann comments:

I audition the motifs and scanned images, when creating a collage of napkins. Cascob *reflects a visit to a favourite camping spot on the Shropshire/Welsh border. (The pages had been prepared using gesso, acrylic paint and text stamps to represent the spring colours in Welsh border country.) Once the auditioning of motifs is complete, I cut through all three layers of the napkin; the thinner top layer or layers are then applied to the cloth using Art Van Go acrylic wax – the perfect product for allowing the background to show through, [as] the napkin images become almost transparent. [This would be] ideal for travel journals with maps as a base.*

Above Ann Somerset Miles, *Cascob*, 2013. Napkin motifs were affixed to a travel journal map page using Art Van Go acrylic wax – when dry, the map details are still legible.

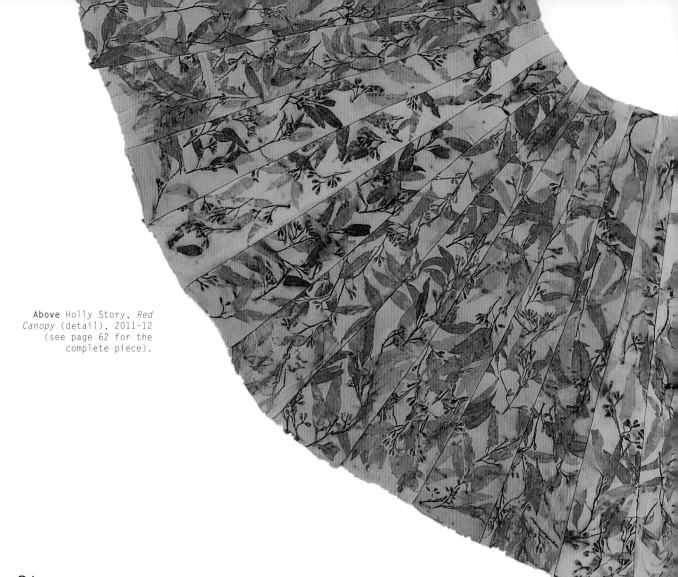

Above Holly Story, *Red Canopy* (detail), 2011-12 (see page 62 for the complete piece).

Holly Story

Holly Story is a visual artist based in Fremantle, South West Australia. Over the past two decades, her art practice has included printmaking, embroidery, installation, video and sculpture. Her work is concerned with human perception, the lived experience, and in particular the interdependence of the human and natural world. At the heart of her practice is a 30-year relationship with her research site on the Deep River, on the south coast of Western Australia. It is here, in a wild place, that she has developed skills in what she refers to as 'listening' to the natural world around her, using all her senses to begin to understand something of the unique rhythms and patterns of relationships that make up the particularity of place.

Holly's work has been described as 'slow art': materials are gathered and used where she is working, as evidenced in the monumental work *Red Canopy* (2011–12). Over the course of 12 months she went on numerous walks along the track leading through the forest near her studio at Deep River and collected karri (*Eucalyptus diversicolor*) leaves and buds blown down from the canopy. These plants were bundled and wrapped before being steam-printed (in metal containers) on to a series of panels cut from second-hand wool blankets. The blankets were then hand-stitched into a large ring. The intense red, vermilion and orange leaf patterns obtained through the dyeing process reflect and reference the leaves she saw overhead in the bush, and the broken light shining through the stands of eucalyptus trees.

The work appeared for the first time at the exhibition 'Look Both Ways' at the Turner Galleries, Perth, Western Australia, in 2012. The artist Gregory Pryor wrote :

Here we are prompted to look above and below us as if the artist is leading us through her own navigation of the bush. The hole in the centre of this canopy could be for the trunk of one of the karri trees contributing to this work, but when we turn around in the gallery to view the video work Spin, *we see that this space is occupied by a woman who wears the 'canopy' like an enormous skirt, spinning around to reanimate the leaves again. The camera only focuses on the spinning skirt, with an occasional glimpse of feminine legs, but it is a significant figurative presence for this artist, who has previously only alluded to it or consciously addressed its absence.*

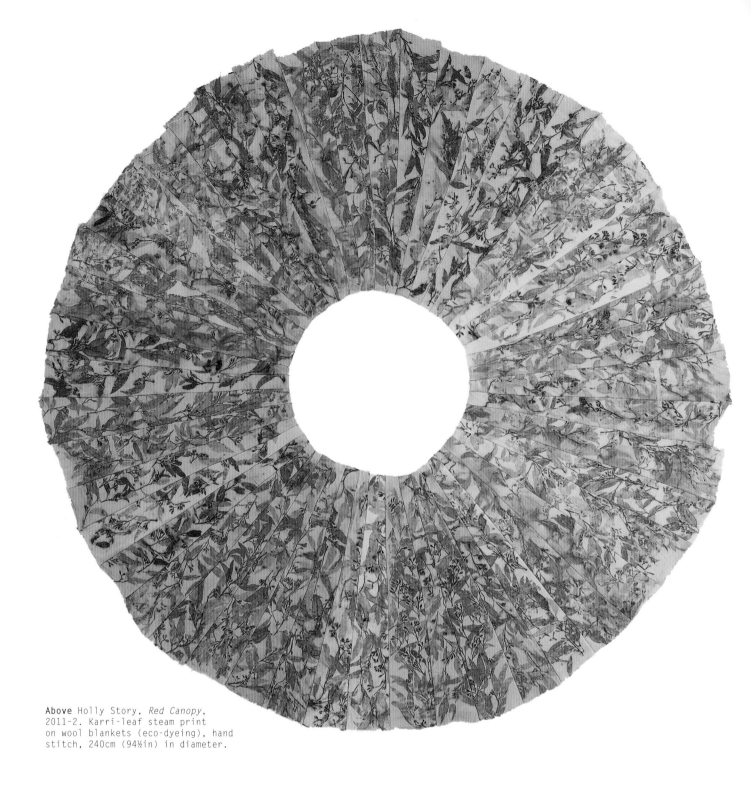

Above Holly Story, *Red Canopy*,
2011-2. Karri-leaf steam print
on wool blankets (eco-dyeing), hand
stitch, 240cm (94½in) in diameter.

By using materials collected from the sites of her investigations, Holly invokes the place in the work, and by using simple and traditional textile practices she grounds the work in the everyday of human history, adding weight to her understanding that we should not think of ourselves as set apart from the world we live in, in the hope that this change of perception will go some way toward restoring a balance in our dealings with the natural world.

Red Canopy marked an important shift in Holly's practice. The use of a video in the gallery installation to depict the wearing of the skirt/artwork as a kind of ritual garment engages us in a role of 'sympathetic magic' between the wearer, the wind and the trees.

Eco dyeing

The process described in Holly's work is commonly known as eco dyeing. It is an ecologically sustainable process using renewable plant resources to imprint colour and patterns from leaves, flowers and seedpods on to (mostly) wool and silk-based cloth. Artists choose their own methods and ingredients based on what works for them, but usually the cloth and plants are wrapped around metal rods, wood or stones (or folded/bundled together), ensuring that the plants have contact with the cloth's surface. This is then steamed or placed in boiling water in a metal container or pot for 60 minutes or longer.

Different metal pots – iron, copper etc. – act as a mordant, altering the colour of the plants. Some artists also use alum and cream of tartar as a mordant. Ideally, the bundles are best left for a few days to 'cure' before unwrapping them. Some people place plant dyestuff, ground-up roots, leaves and so on in a glass jar with the cloth and solar-dye them by leaving the jars in a sunny spot for days or even weeks. India Flint's excellent book *Eco Colour* is the bible for anyone wanting to study the process in great depth.

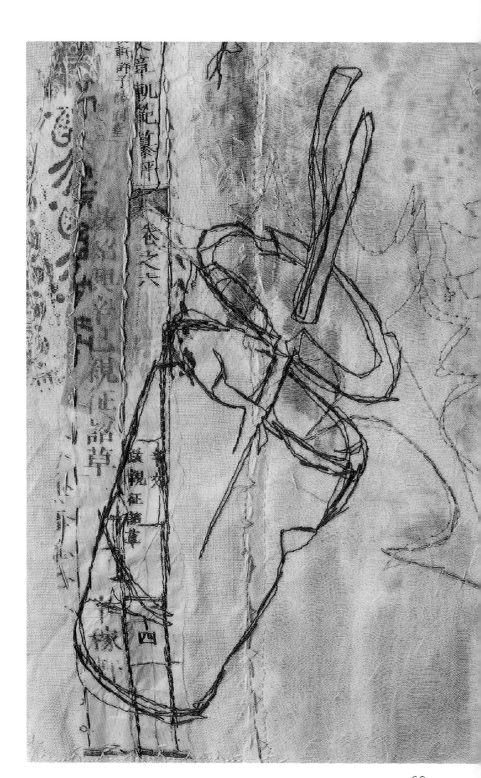

Right *Cup and Dandelion*, 2013, 70 x 58cm (27½ x 23in), machine and hand-stitch details on a background of dyed cloth and found papers and fabric.

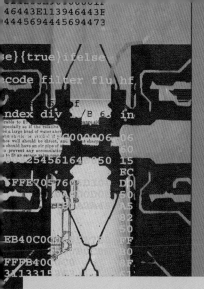

ALL IN THE DETAIL

There is a wealth of rich detail that lies in the everyday world around us if only we take time to look: the places that lie where the urban world meets nature, complex interweaving of the built and the natural in our city and town environments. Intensely detailed and multi-layered, the often overlooked places on the edges of our vision, the edges of footpaths, urban walls and building sites are places which plants and wildlife inhabit. The colours, texture and changing light provide an intricate visual resource for the textile artist readable on a number of levels.

40 Yards

Creating work with limited resources sometimes leads to unexpected outcomes. Making, travelling, teaching and writing is a juggling act, and when I had some building work done at home, my stash of materials had to go into storage and was inaccessible, and space was at a premium. This presented a challenge when I was invited to create an exhibition – 'Spaces, Places and Traces' – for the 20th European Patchwork Meeting.

I found a scrap of fabric on a local footpath with '40 yards' printed on it: this was a start. I decided that I would reflect the various seasonal changes and daily observations I made of the street, gardens and park near my home (within 40 yards) in an ongoing 'diary' piece. The basis of the work was to use whatever materials (paper and cloth) I could gather whilst travelling, or which had been donated by friends, combined with whatever I had to hand for mark-making, drawing and stitch.

Working with these restrictions on my space and time only allowed me fleeting glimpses of the work in progress as

a whole. As I worked, I became aware of how the materials collected reflected the patterns, colours and changes I saw around me in nature. The pieces acted like stops on a journey or snapshots of a given time, connecting time spent away travelling and working to the more intimate and familiar space of home. The commonality of things acted as inspiration – things I saw that were familiar but different, such as lace curtains in a window with a view on to a different location, or a flooded garden, or a park in winter. Perhaps I was actively seeking botanical forms, birds and small details as a focus of calm amidst the disruption of my time and personal space.

The installation of the pieces was equally dictated by time and space, as I had less than a day to set it up. I decided to line up the work chronologically, making small adjustments as the space dictated. The converted performance space of La Mine D'Artgent in Sainte-Marie-aux-Mines, France, was an ideal space. It was flooded with overhead light, which allowed the work to float on the walls. The usage of material exposed another narrative, as a section of lace or seam from a shirt became revealed from one of the pieces to another in the sequence.

Left *Cup and Dandelion* in progress on my studio wall (see page 63 for a detail of this piece).

Right *Kitchen Goddess and Roses*. Detail of a piece demonstrating machine and hand stitch onto a domestic tea towel (see page 79 for the complete piece).

Above *40 Yards*. View of part of the installation at the European Patchwork Meeting in Alsace.

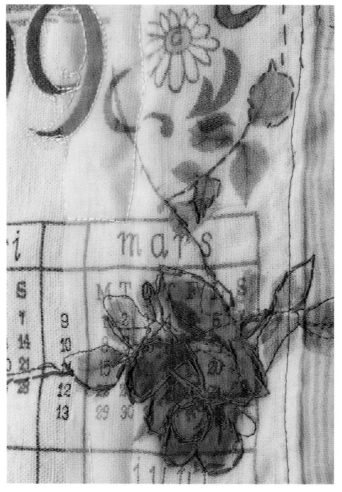

67

Plant blindness

Australian artist Christine Atkins creates mixed-media pieces exploring the concept that we no longer see the natural world and its changes in our busy lives. She makes reference to James Wandersee and Elisabeth Schussler (1998) who propose that 'we have become so disconnected and removed from nature that we no longer see the plants around us'. They have named this phenomenon as 'plant blindness'.

Christine asks whether we really see seasonal changes such as trees coming into flower, or whether we are too immersed in planning our day and getting to work to take any notice. Her work asks us to consider the small details of life and rediscover the plant life that surrounds us. She begins with a found object such as a single leaf, seedpod or bone, and each becomes more than an inanimate object used to create an aesthetically pleasing image. Each object has a sense of history, an imagined story. Combining metal, timber and fibre, a gathered stick becomes a tree, a home for a bird to nest.

Her intricate, detailed pieces are worked in sculptural stitch combined with cast metal, wood and found objects and pay tribute to the many ways that plants enhance our lives, from their serious and life-sustaining properties to sheer visual and scented pleasure.

Left Christine Atkins, *Before Beginning Your Journey*, 2012, 42 x 50 x 10cm (16½ x 20 x 4in). Wording on it reads 'Before beginning your journey pack all that is precious'. Machine embroidery, hand stitching, salvaged timber, hand-carved timber, found objects.

Right Christine Atkins, *Finding Home* (detail) 2011,180 x 104 x 24cm (71 x 55 x 10in). Wording on work reads, 'Leaves rustling, standing tall, after the storm. Wanting to find home. Quiet the beating heart, move in silence, to hear the trees whispering song to guide you home. Graceful in the wind, growing strong'. Machine embroidery, hand stitching, thread, onion weed (or 'Guildford grass'), etched brass, found objects.

Grids and patterns in the built environment

Anne Kelly

A found object or scrap of fabric can lead artist Anne Kelly to the creation of intimate textile narratives that include complex layers and richly worked detail. The layers twist and undulate as the stitching creates both physical and visual movement in the newly constructed textile collages. Trapped between the layers you find small details, such as a bird resting on a branch, or a piece of floral fabric, to create interest and texture. Anne's work is informed by her close observations of things she happens upon in daily life and discovers anew.

    Silver Lining contains all of Anne's signature themes and techniques. Images and prints are worked into heavily

appliquéd, machine-stitched surfaces, which are further worked with dense overstitching and hand embroidery. The subject matter and design have a naive appearance, which reflects the rich traditions and qualities of folk art.

Above Anne Kelly, *Silver Lining* (detail) 2011, 85 x 60cm 33½ x 23½in). This richly worked mixed-media textile celebrates the natural world in printed images and text combined with the details to be found in the reworking of the rich vintage fabrics.

Rosalind Davis

Rosalind Davis's mixed-media oil paintings reflect architecture and the built environment. She often uses domestic fabrics or patterned cloth as a ground, and incorporates stitch and thread. Through this materiality, she questions the stereotypical perception that embroidery is a safe, feminine craft, conjuring up connections to the domestic, the tactile and the handmade. This lies in opposition to the architecture represented in her artworks (often sourced from images of 1950s modernist buildings and interiors), which is largely seen as a masculine domain. (Typically, few women were recognized, represented or celebrated within modernist art or architecture.) Rosalind comments:

As a woman exploring modernism in my work, the needle and thread inherent in the works are also a symbolic gesture, of piercing and puncturing the perceived limitations of sexual stereotyping. It is a feminist gesture (as well as a reparative gesture) and used as a tool to reinterpret modernist spaces, to reflect a feminine intervention as well as piercing historical stereotypes about the undermined roles of women in the cultural landscape of art, art history and architecture.

Embroidery is utilized as a human and emotional connection between environment and landscape, emphasizing the humanity and fragility of these depicted spaces as well, conjoining both masculinity (painting and architecture) and femininity (embroidery and interior domestic space) and emphasizing their coexistence.

The painter (and her former tutor) Graham Crowley said about her work: 'Rosalind creates a tension between embellishment and depiction, sensuality and awkwardness, shifting the decorative aspects and the tradition of embroidery. The nature of embroidery dictates that the surface of her paintings becomes heightened by the physicality of the stitching.' The works explore issues such as the current economic crisis, exports, and manufacturing and trade in the UK, emphasized through the symbolic use of both fabric and embroidery.

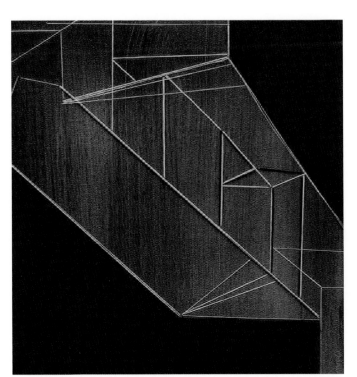

Left Rosalind Davis, *Unveil*, 2013. Oil and embroidery on linen, 30 x 30cm (12 x 12in). The stitch literally 'punches' the surface of the painted canvas.

Above Rosalind Davis, *Ardwick*, 2011. Oil and embroidery on cotton, 70 x 95cm (27½ x 37in). Toile de Jouy was used as a base for painting and stitch representations of the modernist buildings in Ardwick (an area in Manchester that used to have a thriving textile industry in the 1900s).

Eszter Bornemisza

Hungarian artist Eszter Bornemisza reflects our relationship to the traces and settlements of past and modern cultures. City plans and maps are excavated out of newspaper and cloth, with regular rhythms and patterns that reflect Eszter's earlier training in mathematics.

A more radical form of her earlier explorations into cut-back appliqué, the base materials of reprinted newspaper, maps and found paper have been layered with discarded threads and yarns or even catgut in netted and dimensionally shaped pieces. In *Lung of the City,* some pieces float within three transparent panels showing fragments of a Budapest map, to varied scales. The piece, in a rich palette of gold, rust and grey, overstitched with bold red circles and meandering lines, looks at present-day changes to Budapest and reflects Eszter's concerns about urban sprawl:

The red holes indicate the parks and green areas, often referred to as the lung of the city. As sizes of holes are getting smaller with zooming in, I intended to express my growing concern about the recent year's rush of development in the city where I live: greater and greater areas of the hills and forests are being turned to residential areas, while trees in the existing parks are dying out due to the high air pollution.

Below Eszter Bornemisza, *Lung of the City*, 2011. 300 x 100 x 80cm (118 x 39 x 31½in). Newspaper and ripped map fragments held on an open-weave base, overprinted, dyed and then stitched.

Neil Bottle

Sometimes a textile may be informed by the texture and marks we associate with cloth, but may contain no stitch. In the 20 years since he won the Painter-Stainers' award for printed textiles, artist Neil Bottle now works on large, richly coloured pieces using digital textile printing. He is an experienced silkscreen printmaker and translates his new work with such detail and texture that, on first glance, the surfaces of the panels give the illusion of being both printed and stitched.

The combination of new forms of printing with Bottle's unique design approach is best described in this review by Sue Prichard:

In many ways these exuberant textiles reflect both the artist's personality and his practice – an eclectic mix of architectural and geometric influences combined with signs and symbols underpinned by textual homage to the passing of time. This mix is perhaps a reflection of Bottle's decision to site his design studio on the East Kent coast – an area where the tensions created between elemental landscape and urban regeneration combine to create a harmonious whole personified by his unique and limited-edition textiles.

(SUE PRICHARD, 2010)

Prichard continues: 'The subtlety of the design … [reveals] a complex hidden narrative of words and numbers which stir memories of the futuristic world of The Matrix'.

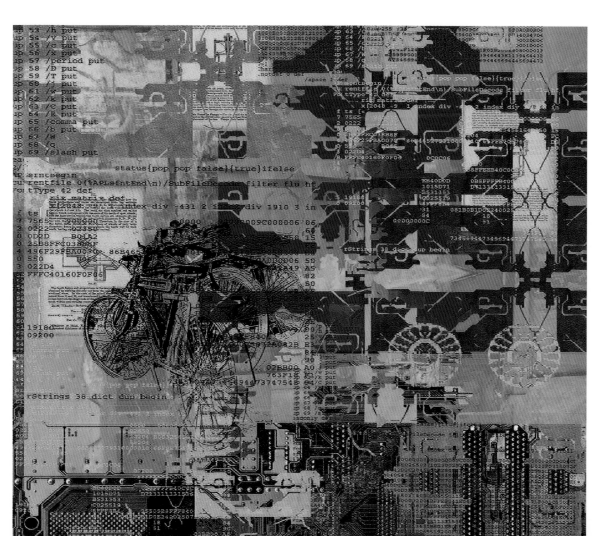

Left Neil Bottle, *Blue*, 2010, 60 x 60cm (23½ x 23½in). Hand- and computer-generated images, digital-printed cotton sateen wall hanging. Technocraft Collection.

Within your footsteps

Items gathered as part of a journey, holiday or visit to a special place can provide inspiration. Old postcards, maps and tickets carry their own memories of place and time. Sometimes, forgotten postal items lurking at the back of a drawer, in a pocket, or found in a charity shop, car-boot fair or flea market carry a particular resonance as a reminder of the past. Will the digital age spell the end of such records?

Below and right *Kentish Weald*, 2013 Folding book form and sketchbook for a touring exhibition, 'Envelope Art', organized by Quilt Star, Germany. Each participating artist incorporated a disused envelope into their artwork.

Peta Lloyd

Australian artist Peta Lloyd makes full use of mail ephemera in her layered prints and book works. The reuse and 'upcycling' of envelopes, letters and stamps as well as fabric, natural materials and found objects forms an integral part of her practice. Her book form *Botanical Goats* was inspired by three poems written by Kristin Hannaford and was exhibited as part of an installation – 'TRACE: Art, Poetry and the Built Environment' in Rockhampton, Australia, in August 2013.

Peta uses a number of print and mark-making processes in her work, including collography, screen printing, and monoprinting with gel plates (which gives a lovely textured feel to the print and allows her to use resists in the form of cut-outs and stencils).

In *Botanical Goats* (see pages 76–77), Peta started with a collection of plain and patterned envelopes, some with windows, and stained many of them with tea. Leaves gathered from beneath a banyan tree near her house and other found papers were added to the stash. She prepared a hand-cut silhouette of a goat as a template for the print.

After printing, several of the leaves and envelopes used in the printing process were stitched to a few pages of the book, providing another tactile layer. A piece of recycled tar paper became the cover, adding textural interest. Peta explains:

I wanted the book to be highly interactive for the viewer; there are three folds … to open in order to see the complete page. A simple pamphlet stitch was used to attach each folio to the cover. My sewing cottons were left untrimmed: they spill from the book, representing hairs from the goats.

The process Peta uses for her monoprints requires a gel plate rather than a glass plate, but the methods are very similar, as Peta describes here:

I use a 'real' gelatine plate (as opposed to a manufactured plate, which doesn't melt and doesn't need to be kept in the fridge); I also use acrylic paints of a good quality. The fact that the gelatine plate is moist helps to keep the acrylic paints 'open' for longer; extender can be added for this purpose as well. You can also use the manufactured Gellie Plates when there is no access to a fridge to set the gelatine; however, I can't get the same detailed results as with the 'real' gelatine plates as the paints dry out very quickly, particularly in the Australian climate. I do love the prints that are produced from the 'real' plates and I love that it is 'kitchen technology' in more ways than one!

How to make a gelatine plate for monoprinting

You will need

- Low-sided plastic or metal tray to use as a mould
- Measuring jug
- Water
- Food-grade gelatine (Dr Oetker leaf gelatine is good)
- Measuring spoon, a spoon, and a whisk
- Small bottle of glycerine
- Cling film

1 Pour water into the mould to work out how much it holds and then pour it back into the measuring jug.

2 Mix up a double-strength mixture of gelatine, following the directions on the packet, for the quantity of water in the jug. Add just a few drops of glycerine to help to preserve the gelatine plate.

3 Scoop off the foam and slowly pour the mixture into the mould. If you would like to lift the gel plate from the tray for printing, you can line the tray with cling film first; alternatively, you can leave the gel plate in the tray, in which case there is no need for cling film.

4 Skim off the remaining bubbles with a piece of newspaper and cover with cling film before placing in a refrigerator for several hours to set (overnight is ideal).

TIP: You can refresh old gelatine by cutting it up into small pieces and liquefying it in a microwave for around three minutes, before pouring it back into the tray.

Printing with a gelatine plate

The process for printing with a gelatine plate can equally be applied to a glass plate, with differing results. The paint will also dry more rapidly as you work.

You will need

- Gelatine plate
- Paints, inks or dyes
- Found objects, leaves, paper cut-outs – anything for texture
- Paper or fabric (washed), cut to size
- Paper towels or cloth to wipe hands and paint jars
- Paintbrush or roller (brayer) to spread paint
- Covered work surface and area for finished prints to dry
- Dry brayer (optional)

1 Cover the gelatine plate with paints, inks or dyes. Place the found objects, cut stencils or leaves on top of the inked plate.

2 Lay the paper or fabric on top of the plate to take the first print. Press gently with the flat of your hand or roll a dry brayer on the back of the paper to get an imprint.

3 Ink up the plate again and reposition the objects, or place new objects on the plate, to take a second print.

4 Natural forms such as leaves or plants work well for printing. You can also press textured objects into the plate before you ink it up, such as cloth, wallpaper or a textured collage glued on to card. By repositioning objects as you work, you can achieve layered prints.

Notes

Peta Lloyd uses acrylic paint for printing, but you can experiment with other mediums such as fabric paint or water-based printing ink. I find that printing ink takes quite a time to dry properly. Acrylic or household emulsion paint is a reasonable, cost-effective alternative. You will need to experiment with the consistency of the paint, depending on the absorbency and the texture of the surface on which you are printing.

A good improvised 'work station' can be made from a thin layer of furnishing or packaging sponge, or an old towel, on which you have placed an old cloth as a drop cloth and a few pages from a newspaper. The added advantage of this is that when the drop cloth is dirty, you have another piece of stained and coloured fabric to use in future projects.

Collography

Collography (derived from the Greek *collo*, glue, or the French *coller*, to glue) is a process in which a print is pulled from a plate with a textured surface. The plate is traditionally built up from elements glued to a base of wood or card in the manner of a collage. You can also stitch elements to thin card or plastic sheeting.

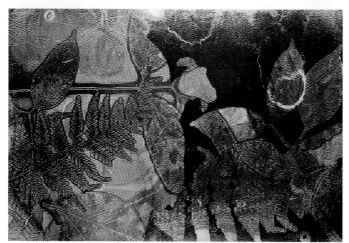

Opposite, far left Gel plate and materials set up ready for the first printing.

Opposite, right First print from the plate showing the goat silhouette and leaves acting as a resist.

Above left Second print from the plate on a new piece of paper. The paper stencil and leaves have been removed. The texture of the leaves have been imprinted into the gel plate surface, leaving a soft residual texture print on the paper.

Left Complex print built up in layers using both residual prints and stencils.

Below Peta Lloyd, *Botanical Goats*, 2013, 30 x 25 x 20cm (12 x 10 x 8in) (closed) Tea-dyed envelopes, mail ephemera, gelatine prints, tar paper, collage, stitch, ficus and gum leaves.

Above Peta Lloyd, *Botanical Goats*, 2013, Open view of one of the pages revealing the addition of machine stitch on top of the collage and printed layers.

Right *Hong Kong Memories*. Folding Book, 2013, 40 x 12 x 14cm (16 x 5 x 5½in).

Below left to right Tin Hau postcard, 14 x 9cm (5½ x 3½in), book cover and half a postcard which was hand-stitched and used as a printing plate on both the book and the postcard.

Books and narrative

Books and narrative-inspired pieces can unfold in many different ways, acting as small 'galleries' of our observations filled with texture and colour. Chronicling a journey or a period of time, the book form can be fluid in its construction and added to as you observe something new. The distinction between paint, paper and cloth becomes blurred when working across different media to develop the pages.

The materials you collect, such as books, maps, postcards or other printed matter, can be deconstructed and reconstructed as they relate to your theme. Parts of your drawings or photographs, pages from reference books and the natural world, or illustrations from stories can be used directly, or scanned and copied (old books are normally out of copyright, which makes them useful for inspiration and reference). Book forms can be small enough to hold in your hand, hung on the wall in modular or folding pieces, or they can become free-standing sculptures.

In *Hong Kong Memories* (above), both the cover and the pages of the book were printed with small stitched circles from a postcard gathered on my travels. This was cut in half to create two hand-stitched printing plates. The same plate was also used on postcard-sized samples made with layered found materials collected in the neighbourhood of Tin Hau and inspired by the local temple and shops.

Niru Reid

For the exhibition 'Everyday Encounters' held at the William Morris Gallery in Walthamstow in 2012–13, Niru Reid made reference to William Morris's belief that art should become part of everyday life – uplifting and inspiring the maker and the eventual owner. The gallery was once his family home, from where he explored the local area. These daily journeys influenced his use of images of nature in his work.

In *Cotton Threads*, Niru identifies that just as in Morris's time, there is a struggle to reconcile aspects of our rapidly changing world: cotton/synthetic; paper/digital; reuse/discard; environment/economy etc. She states:

A place becomes a home from our daily encounters with people and possessions. Similarly, we create a personal landscape as we walk, run, dance or ride through the streets, making contact with people and places.

Niru uses stitching in her work to depict these everyday journeys and connections. Images of objects glimpsed and found during these travels are included in the work: a map of Walthamstow from a discarded A–Z, a pair of trainers depicted in monoprint, a blackbird that sings in the urban landscape. The process of machine- and hand-stitching on a fragile paper map turns it into a material that is stronger, softer and more comforting to touch, as the indecipherable mass of information printed on the page begins to make sense and a personal landscape emerges.

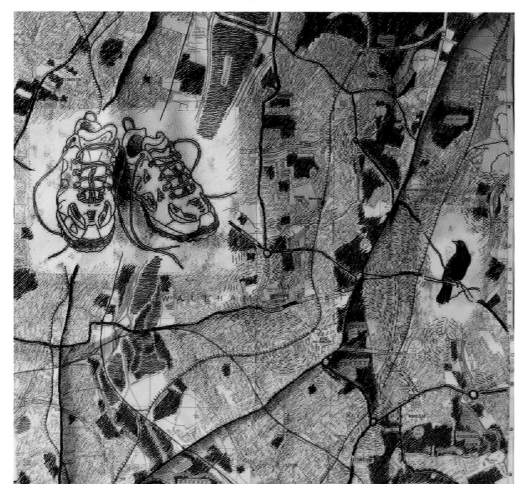

Left Niru Reid, *Cotton Threads*, 2012, 45 x 45cm (18 x 18in). Monoprint, drawing and stitch on an old map.

Above *Kitchen Goddess and Roses*, 2014, 76 x 71cm (30 x 28in). This works uses domestic tea towels as a base overlaid with stitched and painted images of roses. 'The roses – a favourite of my grandmother's – were visible from the kitchen window as she went about her domestic duties'.

OFF THE BEATEN PATH

Textiles have a long tradition commenting on, or being reflective of a particular situation or event. They can explore personal themes and family stories or comment on historical and social narratives. Judy Chicago's iconic feminist artwork, *The Dinner Party* (which I first saw in Islington in the early eighties when an undergraduate) is a compelling example of sociopolitical work. It is a vast triangular table set with 39 places to commemorate 39 women in history. A collaborative work involving hundreds of people (mostly women), each place is set with a ceramic plate, a chalice and beautiful embroidered runners. Chicago demonstrates how 'domestic crafts' can create a different voice in which we can express our ideas. Cloth and stitching has its own narrative tradition to draw from, from the vibrancy of the Suffrage banners in the twentieth century to the more individual, and often hidden, stories of hard work and the domestic responsibilities of family and home.

> I always had the fear of being separated and abandoned. The sewing is my attempt to keep things together and make things whole.
>
> Louise Bourgeois

The artist Louise Bourgeois (1911–2010) drew upon her own unique yet troubled childhood heritage, surrounded by the textiles of her parents' tapestry restoration workshop, for inspiration. Having helped with the repair of items since she was 12 years old, Bourgeois became a lifelong hoarder of clothes and household items such as tablecloths, napkins and bed linen, which she cut up and re-stitched, transforming these familiar materials into art. As Bourgeois demonstrates, textiles bring their own history and cultural traditions to the creative process and this can be used to find new directions and meanings in the creation of work.

Containing evidence of past use, old textiles are a rich source of inspiration, particularly if they have an association with a particular place or conjure up memories of a given time – for example traditional textiles such as embroidered flowers and animals from the Victorian era, or printed floral dress and furnishing patterns. Collections in museums provide a good base for historical research; equally, inspiration can be drawn from our personal histories, family stories and collections:

- A celebration of a family event such as a wedding, or old fabrics that trace the life of a loved one.
- Qualities found in clothing tied up with working lives, from aprons and work clothes to uniforms.
- Folk costumes or clothing worn to mark an occasion.

The choice of materials may reflect a political or social theme. Fragments of vintage textiles, stitched samplers and embroidered household objects reflect the 'domesticity' of stitch. Could their use mark a celebration of the craft, or act as a protest against embroidery being used to keep women 'occupied' in the home, and as indication of a suitable 'feminine' pursuit? Rozsika Parker (1984) notes:

Embroidery was on the one hand expected to be the place where women manifested supposedly natural feminine characteristics: piety, feeling, taste and domestic devotion; and on the other it was the instrument which enabled a woman to obliterate aspects of herself which did not conform to femininity.

Dissenting voices

Artists today are reappropriating the traditions and the feminine associations of needlework and excavating the past to make new statements (and sometimes to express dissent). With the rise of the feminist art movement, embroidery came into its own and arguably became a surprisingly powerful political tool. In the 1980s, large, brightly coloured embroidered banners, echoing the grand traditions of the women's suffrage banners, were carried on marches and hung around the perimeter fences of Greenham Common airbase as part of the Women's Peace Movement. These deliberately evoked the traditions and meanings to be found in embroidery to emphasize that protesters were campaigning as women.

Alke Schmidt

Stitch has become a tool for exploring our relationship with the world and our place in it – a place where issues of social, historical, moral and cultural interest can be discussed. In her 2014 exhibition 'Tangled Yarns' at the William Morris Gallery, artist Alke Schmidt explored the politics and morality of the textile industry and the cotton trade in powerful, often provocative pieces. Her paintings are often intertwined with the decorative patterns of found fabrics, stitch or newsprint, which are chosen for their association with each story being told. Chaos and confusion are clearly evoked in *Aftermath*,

which makes reference to the tragic collapse of the Rana Plaza factory building in Dhaka on 24 April 2013, which killed around 1,138 Bangladeshi garment workers.

The building, which housed five garment factories, was a disaster waiting to happen. Shoddy construction and the unauthorized addition of multiple storeys made it structurally unsound. The death knell for the building – and the people inside – was a power cut causing generators to kick in, adding yet more vibration to the vibration from 1000s of whirring sewing machines. Warning cracks opened up in the building the day before the disaster and concerned workers left. The next day they were ordered back in because their bosses did not want to lose

business for running late with orders. The Rana Plaza factories were, like many others, manufacturing clothes for Western brands.

'TANGLED YARNS' EXHIBITION GUIDE, WILLIAM MORRIS GALLERY, 2014

Above Alke Schmidt, *Aftermath*, 2014, 80 x 100 x 12cm (31½ x 39 x 5in). Found textiles (Walthamstow-sourced fabrics and Western-style clothes made in Bangladesh, as well as shalwar kameez, the traditional South Asian dress that was also worn by the Rana Plaza garment workers), thread, acrylic and sawdust on canvas.

'Extreme stitching'

Machine- and hand-stitched marks are as different as those from a charcoal pencil and a fine drawing pen, and can produce a wide variety of lines. You can exploit their differences: densely worked, the stitched line provides textural interest, or applied in a more open and gestural way, it creates a sense of movement. The sewing machine can be used as a mechanical mark-making tool as you experiment by freely integrating stitch into printed and painted surfaces. (This is a process jokingly referred to by a technician at West Dean, where I regularly teach, as 'extreme stitching'.) The material or cloth equally becomes a 'tool' as well as being a surface for working, as does the texture of the weave, knit or stitch used to make a print or mark.

Although it takes some nerve and can go against the grain to 'dirty' and reuse lovingly stitched pieces of work such as exquisite embroidered linens or remnants of old fabrics, these can be given a new lease of life by adding paint and dye to them. Some of the vintage cloth and stitch details may be almost obliterated through processing, but as the surface dries, new textures and colours are revealed.

Working with vintage materials

Collect a wide range of fabrics, from heavyweight brocades, canvas and calico to lightweight muslins, voiles and silk; think about your inspirational sources as you collect the pieces. Could the colours, surfaces and patterns, as well as their former uses, inform your choice?

• Stitch a selection of the cloth and papers collected into layers using the decorative embroidery settings on your machine, and/or use textural hand stitch. Consider the edges, seams and textures, and crumple, crease and tear different weights of material as you build up the layers. Then try out the following ideas to make a set of samples:

• Dye the newly stitched cloth surfaces in a dye bath (I like to use a low-water immersion method: see page 86) or apply inks or dye with a brush.

Left *Common Place: Marsh Sowthistle*, 2013, 80 x 102cm (31½ x 40in). Pieces of lace are combined with a cross-stitch fragment and reference a love of flora in a familiar landscape, and are a tribute to the intense labour required for the manufacture of lace and embroidered works (both Norwich and the Netherlands once had a thriving lace industry).

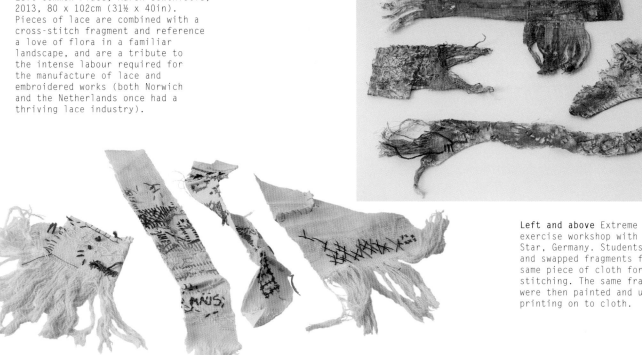

Left and above Extreme stitching exercise workshop with Quilt Star, Germany. Students rotated and swapped fragments from the same piece of cloth for hand stitching. The same fragments were then painted and used for printing on to cloth.

Low-water immersion dyeing

For basic dyeing that requires little in the way of space or facilities and is environmentally conscious, the low-water immersion method is a very satisfying and simple process for dyeing small quantities of fabric.

1 Mix half a teaspoon of Procion MX dye powder with just enough water to make a smooth paste. Add a little more water. This will give a strong solution, which can later be diluted for dip-dyeing and painting.

2 Make up a soda solution (three scant tablespoons of soda ash or nine tablespoons (150–200g/5½–7oz) of washing soda to a litre of hot water). Allow to cool.

3 Place damp, pre-washed fabrics in small plastic containers or jars (ice-cream tubs are perfect). Pour a quantity of the soda solution on to the fabric. Squeeze the fabric to make sure it is soaked through.

4 Add 2–3 tablespoons of the dye solution to the plastic container with the cloth and let it merge gently with the fabric. The more tightly packed the fabric, the more patterning will occur. After an hour, rinse the fabric in cold water until the excess colour runs out and then wash in very hot water, with soap flakes or liquid, by hand.

• Use wax crayons or Markal Paintstiks on the stitched surfaces as a resist before dyeing or staining.

• Cut through layers after working, revealing some of the surfaces underneath.

• Sandpaper the surfaces, fray edges, or pull out threads.

• Use these newly stitched surfaces as collographic printing plates, applying paint on top with a roller or sponge, to create a print from the surface.

• As you work, investigate how the different surfaces respond to the mediums you use. Observe absorbency, dilution, drying times and colour changes. Acrylic and fabric painting/printing mediums will change the handle or feel of the fabric, and the texture or structural patterns in the cloth often become more evident. Transparent mediums, such as silk paints, will allow more of the underlying print pattern to show through. A 'new' fabric can emerge from old cloth with the application of dye or paint, and provide interesting textured backgrounds or surfaces for further development in stitch.

Above: *Norfolk Reeds*, 2014 23 x 30cm (9 x 12in). Backs of tea towels have been painted and distressed. Original stitched seams are evident in the section of a shirt seam. Attached by a paperclip is the fragment of embroidered textile used to print in the background of the stitched reeds.

Right In the foreground are dyed machine-stitched cotton fabrics. Note the polycotton flower stitch detail and machine stitch have not taken the dye. Behind these are paint rags donated by students attending classes.

Safety precautions when using dyes

- Treat all dyeing and some painting materials as poisonous.

- Keep a separate set of utensils for dyeing.

- Cover all work surfaces with protective covers such as newspaper or polythene.

- Wear rubber gloves and wash these well after use.

- Do not inhale the dye powder: it is advisable to wear a mask when handling it. Fibre-reactive dyes can produce asthma-like symptoms in some people; if you have respiratory problems, it is best not to handle them.

- Store the dyes in containers with secure lids and label them very clearly.

- Be careful when using boiling water and corrosive substances such as bleach and washing soda. Spills may make the floor slippery!

- Do not eat or drink in the dyeing area.

Above A small piece of quilted fabric with additional stitch added to create a texture for printing.

Right *Elder* (detail) 2014, 160 x 30cm (63 x 12in). Machine- and hand-stitch motif on a background composed of paint rags and plant-dyed fabrics.

Using family history

Textile work may be autobiographical or biographical, reflecting personal history, stories and the human condition. Artists whose interest lies in items embellished with embroidery and objects handled by other people produce pieces that may be nostalgic in feel, creating a connection between the present and the past.

Sheilagh Dyson has a passion for arts and crafts with a vintage feel, and is drawn to mixed-media techniques that also demonstrate her love of photography. Her use of recycled fabrics, garments, wool, and broken and unloved 'treasures' stems from a make-do-and-mend ethos inherited from her mother (long before the current financial climate made it fashionable). The resulting items of clothing, jewellery-inspired pieces and books combine a practical application with a conceptual approach. She uses image transfer on fabric and mixed-media surfaces to express her ideas of the past in photographic form.

Sheilagh discusses the process behind one of her works:

During my visits to Kent Life (a heritage centre based on the history of farming in Kent), I was drawn to the houses with their carefully chosen furniture and paraphernalia helping to re-create the atmosphere from days gone by. Of particular fascination were the occasional glimpses of the families who once walked those rooms, their ghostly presence marked with a photograph here and there, fixing their image at a moment in time. The idea quickly formed to use this as the basis for my artwork for 'Transpositions'. Suddenly, these ghosts of past residents became more real as I was given access to the extensive archive, carefully collected over the years by the Friends of Kent Life, who have been invaluable in my research.

Whilst the various dwellings at Kent Life have been lovingly restored to their former glory, and in many cases brought back from the brink of destruction and recreated brick by brick, their occupants have, for the most part, been forgotten.

I have chosen the form of a textile/tactile photo album as a means to remember and celebrate some of these past lives, 'fleshing out' the characters who once called Sandling Farmhouse their home.

Photographic image transfer with paint and stitching

The transfer of photographic images or copies of drawings to cloth is a useful process for the textile artist. Use a computer to manipulate digital photographs: you can achieve complex surface designs for stitch by repeating and layering images. It is possible to send designs to commercial firms for printing directly on to the fabric of your choice by the metre. I have found this particularly useful for commissioned work where stability of the image is important.

It is also possible to run fabric straight through a printer at home, since they usually use dye-based printing inks. To achieve a permanent result, paint or pre-soak a smooth fabric

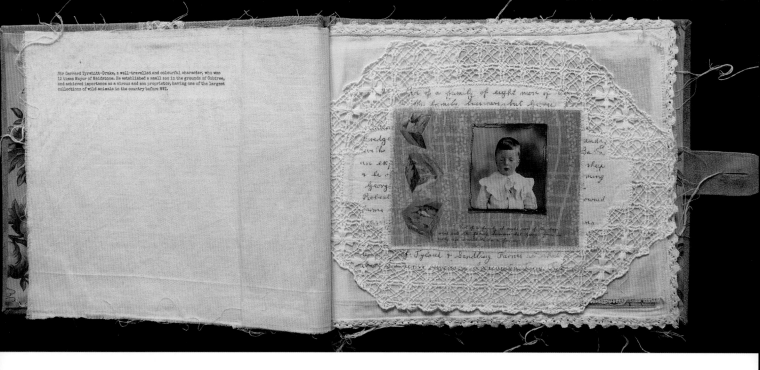

in a liquid medium such as Ink Aid or Bubble Jet Set 2000 and allow it to dry. Cut the fabric to size and iron it on to freezer paper before passing it through the printer. (There are several books on the market that cover a variety of photo- or image-transfer processes in more depth.)

Transfer Artist Paper

Sheilagh Dyson researched image-transfer paper in some detail during her photographic studies, and Transfer Artist Paper (TAP) is one of her recent discoveries. Developed by the artist Lesley Riley in the USA, the concept is similar to the widely available iron-on transfer papers, in that an image is printed in reverse on the TAP paper via an inkjet printer, and ironed on to fabric. The important difference, as far as Sheilagh is concerned, is that the TAP paper uses a polymer coating, enabling the image to be absorbed into the fabric rather than remaining as a plasticized layer. This preserves more of the original 'handle' of the fabric whilst producing clean, sharp, matte images (something that proved frustratingly elusive in Sheilagh's earlier photographic studies!). Authors note: Lesley Riley's TAP paper is no longer available.

During Sheilagh's on-site research for *Sandling Ghosts*, original photographs and other relevant two-dimensional paraphernalia (some dating back to the early nineteenth century) were carefully photographed with a digital SLR camera in order to allow simple post-processing with commercially available software. Digital photos provide a better-quality, higher-resolution image than scanning with a typical home-office flatbed scanner, and taking an image of a document *in situ* reduces the need to handle the original, often precious, artefact.

Left Sheilagh Dyson, *Polka Dotty* (detail).Page from the album. Acrylic inks and a white gel pen were used to accent key features of photos reproduced on satin paper, to link with the vintage buttons, linens and polka-dotted background.

Above Sheilagh Dyson, *Sandling Ghosts*, 2012. 43 x 33 x 2cm (17 x 13 x ¾in). Handmade textile album with 10 pages of cotton cloth, using mixed-media and image-transfer techniques, created from recycled materials. This was created as an installation piece for the exhibition 'Transpositions' at Kent Life, a heritage centre that was formerly a farm.

Sheilagh used TAP paper extensively in the production of an album, to embed printed images directly on to the vintage and recycled linens used to create the pages. To provide textural contrast and allude to the traditional family album, she first printed some of the photos on a satin photographic paper and sprayed them with a fixative that resists ultraviolet light, for improved longevity. These were then spray-tacked (for a temporary fix) and stitched to the background fabric. Other images were transferred to remnants of calico with TAP paper, before adding them to the pages.

Further mixed-media techniques

Sheilagh's re-creation of the traditional family album is given an extra dimension through texture and colour, breathing life into the old photographs and ephemera unearthed in research. She used a variety of non-digital painting and stitch techniques for more variety in the *Sandling Ghosts* album, such as:
• The use of acrylic paints with extender to apply washes to the pages.
• Collages built up of photographic and painted elements. The whole page was then attached to a calico base using gel medium and stitched through at the edges. This provided a soft but durable 'textile' handle to the painted and collaged paper.
• Adding colour to a black-and-white image. A simple inkjet print on satin photographic paper was first soaked for approximately 30 seconds to make the coating slightly more permeable, before applying localized watercolour washes.

I took part in the same 'Transpositions' exhibition at Kent Life. Hop-pickers were known as 'hoppers' and I was drawn to the huts where the hoppers lived, reflecting on the life of my Romany grandmother and generations of her family as they came to work on the hop fields during the century before the Second World War. My great-grandmother would have made the hut homely for her family, furnishing it with fabrics and utensils that were beautiful as well as functional.

My work *Hop-Kins* uses some of the vintage fabrics I remember in my grandmother's home. My portrait image appears as a reflection in the storyboards about the life of the hop-pickers. It was transferred from a photocopy on to closely woven cloth using white acrylic paint as a wet transfer medium. The hops were heat-transferred with disperse dyes on to net curtain as a negative shape (the hop plant was placed between the dye-painted transfer paper and cloth whilst ironing).

Above, left Cas Holmes, *Hop-Kins*, 2012, 4 panels each measuring 160 x 40cm (63 x 16in). The piece is composed of vintage fabric, lace curtains and tranferred images, machine and hand stitched. Above, right *Hop-kins* detail.

Rosie James

Scenes of everyday life and the pastime of people watching can be a rich source of ideas. Artist Rosie James creates studies of people based on her own photographs of them out and about, standing, walking or waiting. Strongly stitched machined lines in the cloth capture and still the movement and character of individuals. She gives her drawings a name drawn from those of her family and acquaintances, in much the same way as a novelist may create a name for a character in order to file and organize the work as it progresses. Below, she describes one person from a crowd walking towards London Bridge Station during the evening rush hour. 'Carol' features in her work *Crowd Cloud*.

This is Carol. She has two bags, one of which has 'Hobbs' written down the side. She holds a pair of glasses in one hand and rummages through her bag with the other. Carol, then, is probably looking for her ticket, and she will probably need her glasses to make sure she has the correct ticket. Carol has just finished work and is on her way home. She managed to pop out at lunchtime and do a bit of shopping and has treated herself to a new skirt from Hobbs. As it is from Hobbs, she probably has a good job that pays well. Those are the guesses and assumptions we can make from these outward signs. I like to think that we are completely wrong.

Rosie works at a large scale so she scales up her drawings and then transfers them to tissue paper. The tissue is laid on fabric (sheers such as silk organza or cotton organdie) and fastened with an embroidery hoop, and then the image is machine-stitched and the thread ends left loose. The tissue can be completely removed or retained. Rosie comments: 'The black line of the thread is a seductive one, raised from the surface it is tactile and slightly fuzzy at the edges; velvety. This is one of the things that draws me to the sewing machine rather than the pencil.'

Right Rosie James, *Crowd Cloud*, 'Carol' (detail), 2011. Installation composed of 20 life-sized stitched drawings of people walking. The transparent cloths were hung from the ceiling in groups of about eight or more so that the viewer could walk around them. Their transparency allows you to see right through, from one person to another.

Rachael Howard

Rachael Howard was one of the first postgraduate students in embroidery at the Royal College of Art (1992). Her graphic textile sketches fix a moment in time in a lively mix of machine stitch and appliqué combined with digitally printed and screen-printed drawings. Her fascination with the everyday world is captured in drawings made almost as if she has 'sneaked up' on her subject unawares.

Rachael may make hundreds of fleeting sketches and will then choose one that best captures the subject in stitch. She explains:

When I am drawing a person I am already, in my mind, thinking about which fabrics I will use to clothe the figure – will it be a satin silk or a patterned cotton? I am thinking about how I will apply the stitching: will I use a set machine-stitch pattern with variegated thread or will it be a simple hand-stitched bead? Fabric and stitch are integral to the expression and life of the drawing.

Above Rachael Howard, *Expecting*, 2011, 70 x 50cm (27½ x 19½in). Silkscreen printing, appliqué and machine stitch.

Mary Fisher

American artist and social activist Mary Fisher references the human condition in her richly patterned quilts containing powerful political messages worked into the intricate layers. Diagnosed HIV-positive in the summer of 1991, she has since worked tirelessly to raise awareness of, and challenge, the stigma about the disease. She is the founder of the Mary Fisher CARE (Clinical AIDS Research and Education) Fund and she also served as an emissary for the Joint United Nations Programme on HIV/AIDS.

Mary balances her passion for art (work in jewellery, painting, weaving, photography and quilting) with her advocacy for those in society, especially women and girls, affected by poverty, violence and AIDS. After seeing her exhibition 'Messages' at the Knitting and Stitching Show in

2013, I was invited to visit her studio in Sedona in the following year. The studio is a testament to an industrious and brilliant mind which, in her own words, 'does not ignore compassion because I am in my studio'. Large dyed, painted, stitched and appliquéd surfaces were strung across a line, and paper stencils were laid on the table beyond, all waiting for her hand to return to the work. It was as if I had stepped into a giant sketchbook or art playroom where the freedom to explore creatively was evident within all that I could see in the space.

In talking about her series 'Faces of My Heart' at the 'Memories and Messages' exhibition, Festival of Quilts, in 2013, Mary discusses how her own memories of individual children she met in Africa, who were orphaned or sick with HIV/AIDS, informed the work:

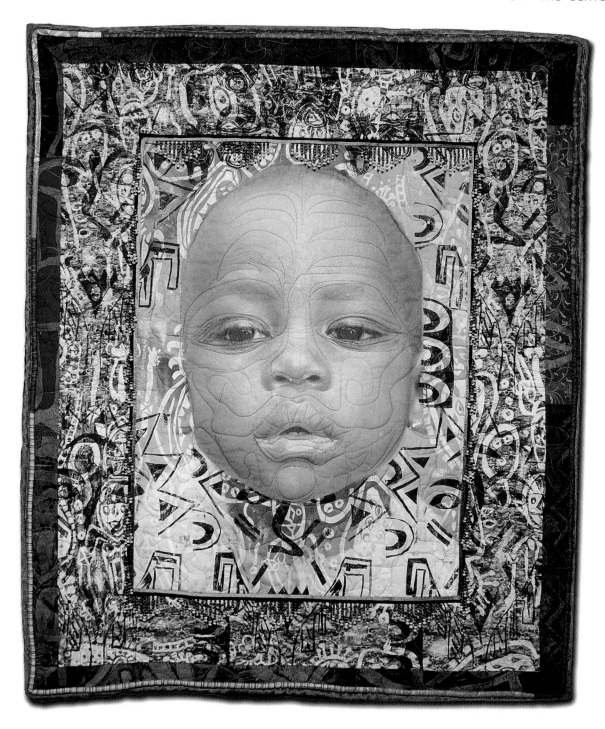

The memories were captured on film by my camera. I wanted to have real photographs of real people because we all risk thinking of 'millions of orphans' as a mass or a concept. They aren't. They are millions and millions of individuals, each one of them a separate, living, dying, gasping child. They are alive and they have names and they have meaning. My fear is that we will ignore their humanity, their individuality.

In speaking of one quilt, *He's My Baby*, she adds:

I wanted this child more than I can say. He was sweet and gentle, his breathing so laboured and his eyes so languid. But I could not move through the bureaucracy fast enough to adopt him, or to save him. As papers were being signed, his laboured breathing stopped. I moved from grace to grief. He is gone now, but he will never escape my memory. I hear him in the night and I reach for him. Then I remember.

Above Mary Fisher, *He's My Baby*, 2013. Art quilt. Photo-transfer on fabric, fabric inks, cotton fabric, block-printing inks, cotton, silk and rayon threads, wool and beading threads, trims, cotton wadding, 119 x 99cm (47 x 39in). Techniques: hand-painted woodcuts and linocuts on cotton, machine and hand appliqué and embellishments, machine and hand embroidery, machine-quilted, hand-painted.

'Talking trash'

Kirsty Whitlock's daily observations are informed by the imagery and text from printed materials she finds when walking down the street or reading a newspaper, or which she collects on a journey. She explains:

My initial ideas often begin from a headline or from the material collected. I am attracted to typography, both handwritten and printed, and colour when collecting items. It could be a shopping list from a shopping trolley or a train ticket which [allows me to] picture a journey. The overlooked surface quality is what catches my eye. The process of experimenting with discarded items and machine embroidery excites me. I love to investigate how materials perform with the sewing machine. If I can sew on it, I usually work with it.

Kirsty's work is conceptual in approach. Time is spent researching the subject, taking notes, recording, drawing, collating and processing ideas in a journalistic or investigative fashion. She develops her initial ideas through experimentation with materials and processes, making samples inspired by the surface qualities of the printed material as well as the subject matter. For example, a combination of plastic carrier bags and machine stitch might be explored through manipulation, layering and fusing.

As part of a continuing process, Kirsty presents her work in a grid format on her studio wall as a means to explore composition, relationships and categories. She uses digital photography and a scanner to record her ideas and to process the found items with collage in her sketchbook. The compositions are achieved by categorizing the discarded items into different types such as typography, numbers and colour types. Kirsty comments:

We are a part of a disposable society that has spread fast through our daily lives. It now seems cheaper to discard items and replace them with new ones. In my 'Talking Trash' collection I exploit the overlooked qualities of discarded household items and aim to critique corporate culture and question society's understandings of value.

The edgy graphic quality in *Bags of Aggro* (shown left) forms part of a series that reflects Kirsty's interest in the increasing visibility of giant supermarket chains both on the high street and in the media, and aims to question what the future holds for us with their rapid growth. She asks: 'Are supermarkets taking over the world?'

Left Kirsty Whitlock, *Bags of Aggro*, 2010, 90 x 70cm (35½ x27½in). Layered and bonded plastic bags, machine stitch.

Right Kirsty Whitlock, 2010, research gatherings. Kirsty catergorizes her gatherings into research grids as part of her investigative process.

YOUR ORDER NUMBER
18

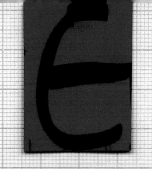

TOKEN 1. TOKEN
12142

M

MISS BETHANY-J.
7 ELDER CLOSE
ARNOLD
NOTTINGHAM
NG5 8GF

FRAGILE

David
6931941

3475

AC 752891
37

Class   Ticket type
STD ANYTIME DAY R
              Start date
              16·FBY·1
From   Va
NOTTINGHAM *   1
To   Ro
LEICESTER *   ANY
              2-

VESTBRIDG-
EICESTER
E3 5BD

2

50p

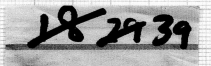
18 29 39

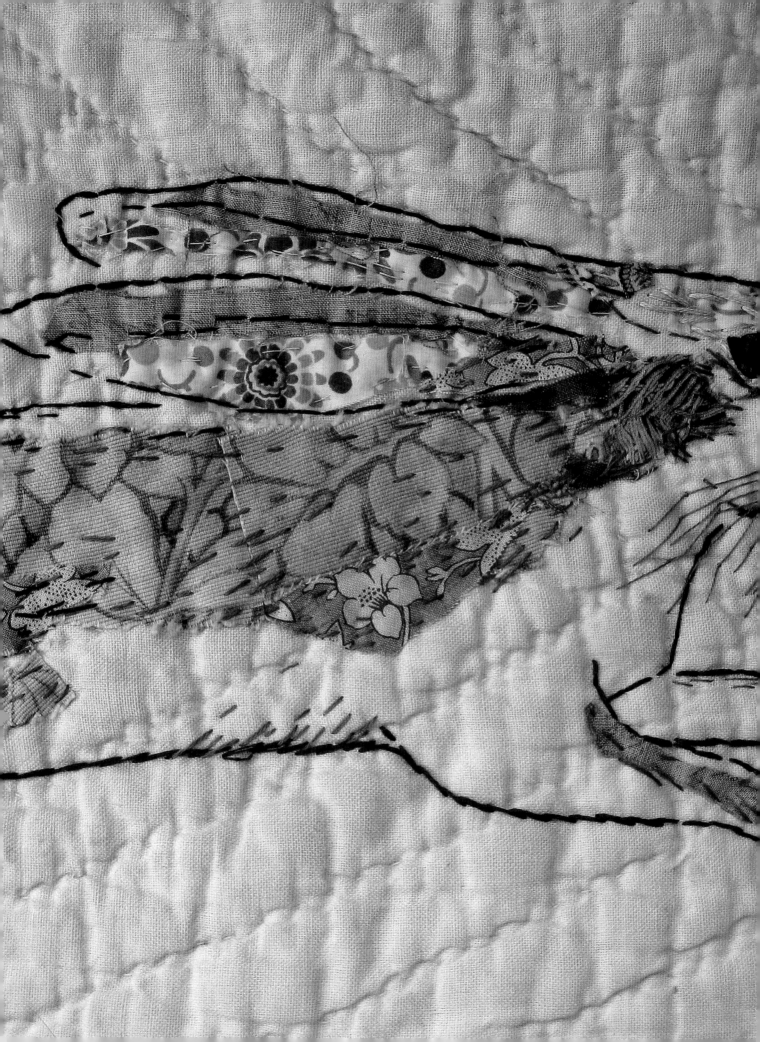

TELLING STORIES IN STITCH

In this chapter we continue the theme of stitch and social narrative in relation to the marks we make on cloth with a focus on the qualities of hand-stitch in relation to machine stitch. In contrast to the seeming rapidity of tools such as the sewing machine in the production of cloth, the use of a needle and thread is slow and more contemplative, and it takes time for work to evolve. Mechanically, the marks are also different. The domestic machine, whilst capable of great speed and diversity in its stitch range, produces a continuous defined line (clearly seen in the work of Rosie James and Rachael Howard), as opposed to softer lines of hand stitching, where the marks are usually broken and more open. The immediacy of hand stitching is the textile artist's equivalent to pencil and sketchpad. All you need is a needle, cloth and thread and you can stitch anywhere.

Stitch signatures

On first appearance, Dutch artist Tilleke Schwarz's work has a strong link to historical samplers. Her pieces make reference to traditional stitches such as cross stitch and couching, and appear to be technically simple; however, Tilleke's use of colour and the combining of threads is far from conventional and is testament to her acute observation of the world around her. She describes her process as more 'intuitive than logical' and talks of 'never planning ahead' and 'just starting to stitch on a piece of cloth':

I use bits of information (texts and images) that I come across from the world and local news, as well as from letters and e-mails I receive. Those texts can inspire me through the meaning or the mere sound of it, or as a metaphor or whatever. I like this information to be combined in different ways – often out of the original context. I choose designs from anything I come across and adjust the colours and composition during the process of stitching. Anything can inspire me. Most important are: folk art (especially samplers), daily news, cats and scraps of textile.

The base for all her pieces is good-quality fine linen (20 threads to a centimetre), which she sometimes dyes. This is worked with all kinds of colourfast threads (cotton, silk, rayon, metallic and synthetic) without using a hoop or frame. Tilleke's graffiti-like stitching reflects many hours of careful observation and drawing and is a subtle comment on what is going on in our world and in our ways of communicating. When I saw her piece *Unfollow*, I asked Tilleke, given the use of the term to describe the 'contemporary problem' of removing unwelcome followers in social media, if it was indeed a reflection of the constraints of, or desire for, mass communication today. She replied: 'Not so much on social media, as I try to stay away from that,' generously followed by 'but I like when people see more things than I put in'.

Tilleke's work resonates with the idea of communication, linking the past with the present and coupling ideas with cloth. In her introduction to Tilleke's book *Making Marks*, Jessica Hemmings states:

Through a cacophony of text and image each [piece of work] continues to build upon the considerable legacy the sampler commands as storyteller. But in place of traditional alphabets or apples are non-linear, postmodern narratives that speak of modern society and the strange way we deal with mass communication.

Right Tilleke Schwarz, *Unfollow*, 2012, 78 x 70cm (31 x 27½in). Hand embroidery on fine linen (50 count, evenweave) with a variety of fine threads (cotton, silk, rayon, polyester and metallic).

Rosalind Wyatt

Rosalind Wyatt's training as a calligrapher before taking up the needle has resulted in wonderfully formed scripts which tie personal narratives into the surfaces of vintage and reclaimed fabric. She completed an MA in textiles and her work is all about words and their relationship to people. She discloses:

My hands become the 'teller' of the tale as I follow the pattern and rhythm of writing. Because the act of stitching is silent and deliberate, it creates a subtle space where you can allow that voice to be heard.

Rosalind is the creative director of a major installation, 'The Stitch Lives of London', in which hats, gloves and clothes are used as a 'canvas' on which to stitch the voices and the words of London's richly peopled history. Rosalind describes how the cloth we wear and the marks we make with a pen carry evidence of a person's identity: 'When text and textile come together, it gives a visceral sense of a human presence'. This is evidenced in the first piece she created, an embroidery on Edwardian silk satin dancing shoes which tells the story of Mary Pearse, the pauper daughter of a London shoemaker. A later piece is worked on the running shirt of the murdered London teenager Stephen Lawrence (donated by his mother, Baroness Lawrence of Clarendon, OBE), titled *The Boy Who Liked to Run*. Stephen's love of running, pride in his achievements and his evident enjoyment of life are what his mother and people close to him remember. Rosalind conveys this through the piece as a celebration of a life well lived, rather than mourning his death. She explains:

Amidst the pages of his drawings and his documents, one stood out. Written on A4 foolscap paper was an A-level essay written a couple of weeks before his death. Stephen left it unfinished mid-sentence. His hand was sure and urgent, with a strong forward slant. These were the words I decided to stitch into Stephen's running top. As both he and his mother were so proud of his sporting achievements, I placed four of his running medals on the front, remade by hand in a textile version, next to his stitched words.

'The Stitch Lives of London' is a major work (still under construction at the time of writing) and has involved a team of people – from stitchers, writers and historians to curators, designers and funders. The installation will be up to 100 metres (394 ft) long and will follow the pattern of the River Thames. It uses 215 pieces of clothing and textile artefacts, each piece marking the length of the river in miles.

Left Rosalind Wyatt, *The Boy Who Liked to Run*, (detail), 2011. This running-top belonged to Stephen Lawrence, who loved to run. It incorporates hand-stitched words and logos of the running club he attended regularly from age 11 to 14.

Above Rosalind Wyatt, *If Shoes Could Talk* (detail), 2011. These beautifully embroidered Edwardian silk dancing shoes tell the story of Mary Pearse, the troubled daughter of a London shoemaker. They were donated by the Ward family from Wandsworth.

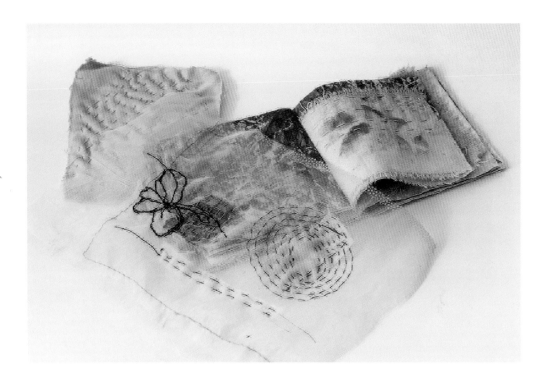

Right Selection of stitch samplers, including a cloth and paper sampler book. Note how the dynamic of straight stitch changes with a sheer fabric and the stitch is visible as a softer line from the back.

Below: Stitch graphics. From the left: irregular straight stitch; couching; diagonal straight stitch with increasing spacing; curved straight stitch; fly stitch and straight stitch; knots and straight stitch.

Making samplers using a variety of cloth surfaces and threads is a good way to explore different approaches to hand stitch. It is also a direct way to introduce gestural line and texture, which reflects the maker's hand or 'signature'.

Try not to plan, but rather react to the material itself. Working with a few of your preferred, or often used, embroidery stitches such as backstitch, French knots or running stitch, invent your own marks based on everyday things. For example you could use ticket details saved from a regular journey, or patterns and shapes based on signs, logos and trademarks collected from places you visit.

Consider the surface qualities of the simple backgrounds found in canvas, calico or linen and experiment with different colours and weights of thread. Manipulate the fabric and explore different methods of attachment and piecing. Include non-traditional materials, pull threads from the weave, tie things off, leave loose ends, or fold and pleat work to add an extra textural dimension. This enables you to develop a visual and physical response to your ideas in respect to the marks you make and the different feel they leave in the cloth.

James Hunting

Artist James Hunting refers to his process of working as engaging with 'the emotion of the stitch'. James has been exploring and developing his understanding of stitch and textile media since graduating in 1986. He talks about the legacy of hand stitch in particular as being 'hidebound' and 'prejudged' by the historical legacy that encourages focusing on technique rather than expression in the mark:

There is a tendency to focus on technique and the visual demonstration of historically misunderstood accepted norms

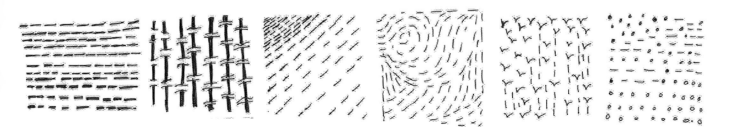

of process. The 'understanding' I talk about goes beyond the technical reproduction of acknowledged named stitches and is an exploration of the emotional and gestural effect one can achieve using needle and thread. I do not 'draw with the needle', a phrase which I believe belittles the act of stitch, but I use the physicality – the interaction of cloth, needle, gesture and brain – a very different act to laying down marks on an often inert substrate. If the viewer's first response to a piece of work is 'What stitch is that?', or 'How did you do that?' then the piece is a failure. I want the first reaction to be 'What is he saying?' or 'That makes me feel/think/sense ...'

James draws upon personal experiences, desires and 'memory codes' in which the work is not explicit in content, but suggestive and acts as an invitation:

The male form is present in my work as an object of desire. Often features are missing, [but] I know who they are; the viewer can bring their own characters to the piece. I have an almost physical hatred of the word 'nostalgia': to me it is a negation of reality and an easily used word conjuring up a domestic utopia that never existed. Memories, however, are painful, embarrassing [and] uncomfortable, but they make us and cannot be ignored. They guide my work. The act of making and ... the joining of the fabrics with embroidery enables me to relive, think and contextualize my life. Once the piece[s] ... [are] completed, my relationship with them changes. They become visually responsible: are they pleasing to the eye? Do they draw the viewer back again and again?

The pieces are layers of life, mine and the viewer's, and are worked as such ...

James works directly on to the cloth. He adds or removes colours and layers as he works, leaving traces of the threads he removes still evident in the surface marks.

Below James Hunting, *And There Will Be Your Heart Also*, 2012, 75 x 60cm (29½ x 24in). Vintage and found fabrics, hand stitch.

Right *Lace Weeds*, 2014. Four pieces each 110 x 12cm (43 x 5in). Stitched and distressed surfaces incorporating lace, fragments from a book on lacemaking, conservation tissue and curtain fabric. The handstitch details include curving running stitch and French knots.

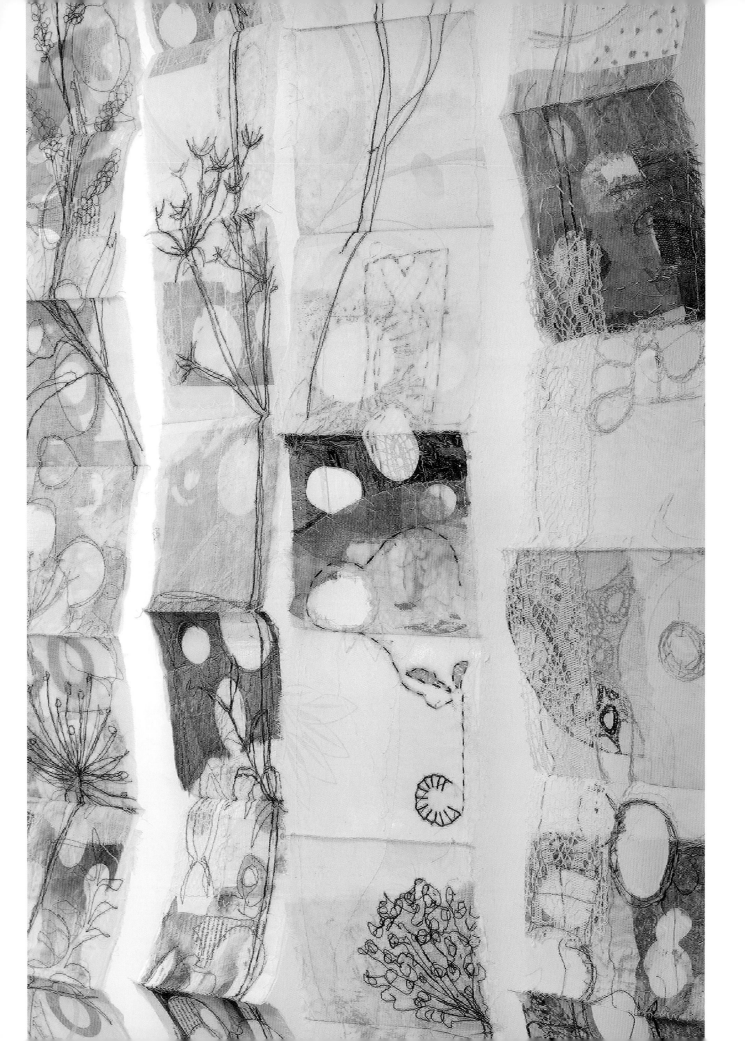

Traditional
stitching methods

The development of a personal approach to hand stitching can be informed by the study of traditional stitching methods, in much the same way as a painter learns techniques through exploration of the work of the masters. Research into traditional folk textiles will reveal stitching methods that can be adapted to fit in with your approach.

My lexicon of hand stitches is small and tends to consist of variations on straight stitches, couching and seed stitch. I will often work on top of a machine stitch to extend and give more weight to a line, or restitch the ends of threads back into a piece. My approaches have been informed by studying the culture and textile traditions of India and Japan, and other places I travel to for work and leisure. When I look at historical or old textiles I am often as drawn to the 'wrong side' of the work – to look at the unobserved or unregarded marks for inspiration and insight into how they were made – as I am to the face of the work.

The traditional use of hand stitch to give a new lease of life to old or worn textiles was born out of necessity at a time when purchasing or making cloth was both expensive and time-consuming. Before the age of the sewing machine, sewers would have used a basic running stitch to hold seams and layers together when making quilts and clothing. The distinctive style of the quilts of Gee's Bend, Alabama, is noted for their lively improvisation and geometric simplicity. These are now highly collectible and have been shown at the Museum of Fine Arts, Houston and the Whitney Museum of American Art, but their heritage is in nineteenth-century slavery and usage for many years into the twentieth century, as women from the black community pieced together cloth to keep their families warm in unheated shacks.

This idea of 'make do and mend', or being thrifty continued. During the years of the Great Depression and through to the Second World War, many homes in the USA and UK were furnished with quilts made with scraps of old or reused material such as furnishing fabric or old clothes, evidencing the maker's life or home. In the USA, women made clothes out of old sacks used for animal feed, flour or sugar. Enterprising manufacturers later printed these with colourful designs for that very purpose.

Mandy Pattullo

The usage of old textiles gives them a new lease of life and asks us to look again at the marks that have gone before. Textile artist Mandy Pattullo recycles vintage fabrics and old quilts into her own work and is particularly interested in pieces that

Above Michigan Quilt c.1940s. Patterned, pieced fabric with sugar-sack backing. Collection of Anna Mansil.

show a history of use, evidencing a previous needlewoman. She often works on both the back and front of pieces, incorporating fragments of cloth, worn edges and pieces of vintage stitch into the work. She comments: 'I don't want to buy new any more and pursue what I call a thread and thrift vision. I primarily hand-sew, combining piecing and appliqué with stitch, and collage in found objects and small, precious bits of embroidery.'

Through stitch, her pieces are connected to time, memory and 'absence' – the evidence of previous hands. This is carried through to her recording processes, in which found materials are incorporated into drawings and collages, found books and related objects.

Above Mandy Pattullo, *Memento Mori*, 2009. Works made with found books and wallets as part of a body of work created in response to the Victorian cemeteries in Jesmond, Newcastle upon Tyne. They include tranfer prints, text and stitch.

Right Mandy Pattullo, *Hare* from the series 'Enchanted Forest', 2013. 20 x 30cm (8 x 12in). The hare is appliquéd on the back of a vintage quilted fragment.

Too good to waste:
kantha, sashiko and boro

The charm of reuse is not in the fashionable re-purposed items of textiles we use in our homes or wear on our person, or even its eco-friendliness. Sewn together over generations, these items also represent the stories and lives of the families who used the fabrics and reveal to us the value of time spent, not money. Most of the stitch techniques employed to recycle and patch cloth were based on simple forms of straight or running stitch, the main component of many traditional embroidery techniques in use all over the world, including kantha from India and Bangladesh, and Japanese sashiko quilted garments and covers.

'Boro' (which translates as rags or scraps of cloth) was a form of peasant clothing which originated in seventeenth century Japan. The word is now used to describe clothes and household items which have been patched up and repaired many times with hand stitch. Born out of the necessary values of 'mottainai' (too good to waste), boro is now valued as an art form and has become highly collectible.

Sashiko

Sashiko quilting originated in the north-west region of Japan and was traditionally worn by farmers, fishermen and their families. The stitching used in sashiko extended the life of indigo-dyed cloth and later, when cotton wadding became available, produced an extremely durable fabric. The value of this fabric was recognized by firemen, who used it in protective coats which they soaked with water before fighting fires. Both functional and beautiful, the coats were decorated with popular geometric motifs such as the hemp leaf or bamboo. Sashiko was later adapted by all classes for clothing. Another variation, hitomezashi, which required only one measured stitch in any direction, was used to create intricate designs.

Kantha

In Sanskrit, the word 'kantha' simply means 'rags'. The term is used to refer to a type of embroidery used to hold pieces of old fabric together. In Bangladesh, women stitched not only out of necessity but also because it was believed that old cloth keeps the wearer safe from harm. The stitching on the cloth gives it a slightly wrinkled, wavy effect and it is typically worked in stacked layers of old saris and cloth to make a light throw or a quilted bedspread.

The colourful embroidered patterns and designs are known as nakshi kantha, a term derived from the Bengali word naksha, which refers to artistic patterns. The best examples employ beautiful motifs of flowers, birds, animals and geometrical shapes to cover an entire cloth. The stitch motifs are usually worked from available patterns and stitched freehand with a traditional dorukha stitch: stitches are of equal length and the design is double-faced. Sometimes one side features a longer stitch than the other.

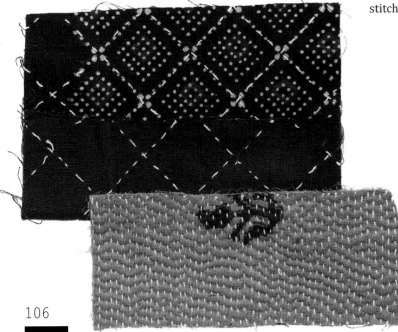

Left Indigo-dyed and printed sashiko with white sashiko stitch, fragment of kantha with running stitch. Collection of Cas Holmes.

Opposite Early twentieth-century Japanese futon cover demonstrating remnants of cloth joined together and quilted with straight stitch (detail). By kind permission of Louis Nierijnck, Maastricht, the Netherlands.

Experimenting with sashiko and kantha

The following exercise has been adapted from the traditional ideas of sashiko and kantha, and uses paper and/or fabric as a base. Look for fabrics and papers that have a colour theme, or which are related in subject – such as floral or geometric pieces. You will be working with stitch through several layers and different weights of cloth and paper. Soft papers such as handmade oriental papers with long fibres, Japanese momigami (strengthened crinkled paper), and lightweight woven fabrics such as cotton and linen, which have been worn and washed many times, work well for this process.

Design your own pattern or download one free from the Internet. To transfer the design to the cloth, you will need chalk, textile carbon paper or an erasable fabric marker (water-erasable pens wash out; lines drawn with an air-erasable pen vanish after a certain period of time). If you are working on the back, a pencil or pen will do instead. For the stitching, a long needle will help you keep the rows of stitching straight. Olympus and Clover make specialist sashiko needles; alternatively, a large embroidery crewel will do. For sashiko, a specialist white or cream sashiko thread is traditional in Japan, but you can use perlé cotton or crochet threads, or experiment with your own collected threads for different effects.

In sashiko, traditional geometric designs featuring interlocking lines, stars, squares, triangles and circles are marked out on the front of the cloth with chalk to provide a guide. The space in between each stitch is half the length of a full stitch. Designs for a sashiko-inspired pattern can also be worked from the back of the cloth.

Below Neil Bottle, *Kantha Blue*, 2014. Detail of geometric digital print with Kantha-inspired stitched motifs.

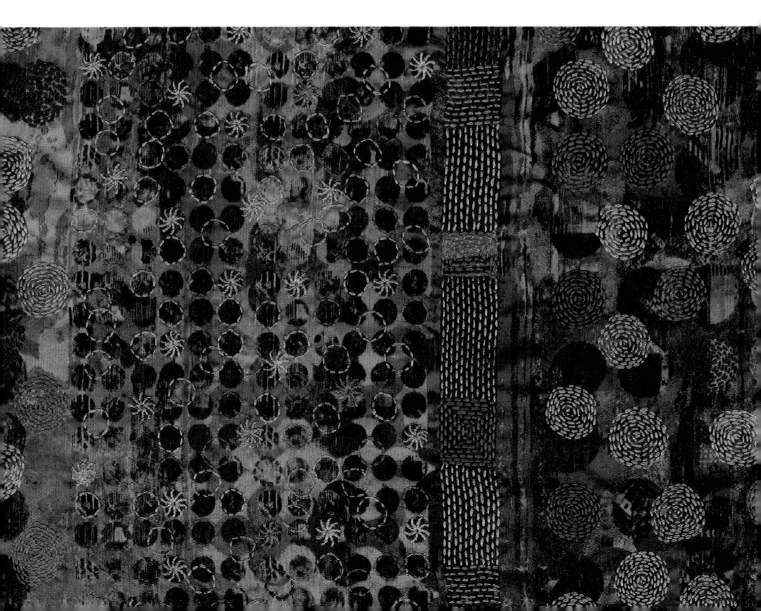

You will need

- A pattern
- Fabrics and papers
- Long, sharp needles
- Medium-weight thread in a colour of your choice
- Scissors or thread snips
- Erasable fabric marker, chalk or dressmaker's carbon paper
- Quilter's rule — imperial or metric, or an ordinary ruler
- Fusible lightweight white non-woven interfacing

To work a design on the front of the cloth:

1 Pin the layers of fabric and paper together and hold with a loose running stitch.

2 Mark your design on to the cloth with chalk or textile carbon paper. A ruler will help with regular lines.

3 Stitch with small, straight stitches following your marked lines as you go.

4 Remove the running stitch.

5 Gently wash the stitched fabric and iron when dry.

   You can purchase traditional Sashiko stencils, pre-marked indigo cotton, marking materials and other supplies on line.

To work a design from the back of the cloth:

1 Pin the layers of fabric and paper together as above.

2 Mark the design on to paper and then tape a piece of fusible interfacing over it.

3 Trace the design on to the interfacing using a permanent ink pen.

4 Iron the fusible interfacing on to the back of the layered fabric.

5 Work the stitching design from the back.

HINT: when working on a geometric design, leave a slack bit of thread when you turn a corner, to prevent pulling.

Above *Imperfect Plant*, 2012, 30 x 24cm (12 x 10in). Black monoprint of plant on muslin with layered muslin and linen kantha stitch on the left-hand side.

Below Kantha in calico and then painted; sashiko on crumpled and dyed paper with crumpled magazine detail; back of brown-paper sample demonstrating marked-out pattern.

Other things to try

You can, of course, make it up as you go and explore running stitch with different weights of thread, varying stitch lengths and multiple colours. Try some of the following:

- Contrasting thread colours and tones; black on white.

- Large, short and uneven stitches.

- Fill the stitched line with backstitch, or another row of running stitch in a different colour.

- Scatter the stitches, making them more dense in one area than another to imply texture and movement.

- Create curved lines, circles, squares, regular and irregular shapes with your stitches.

- Fill in background spaces with stitch.

- Pull the stitches tighter in one area than in another to create strong ripples.

109

LV21: a site-specific artwork

It is an interesting and sometimes challenging dynamic for the working process to develop and evolve ideas in relation to a physical environment, an urban space, or a place in which people work. Referencing, documenting and creating an archive of the evolution of a subject is a process that I became involved with during the restoration of LV21, a 40m (131ft) steel-hulled lightship with an individual and distinct identity.

The ship now acts as a venue for cultural activities across a wide range of artistic disciplines in the Medway area and beyond. It is owned by Päivi Seppälä ('the captain'), who is an artist and has managed a number of high-profile public art projects, and Gary Weston ('the skipper'), an independent film-maker and photographer. In its restoration they have celebrated the maritime traditions of the vessel through the use of environmentally sound processes, from the reuse and sourcing of sustainable materials to building in solar-powered lighting and heating for the vessel's future creative use.

I was given access to the ship to take photographs, make drawings and collect found materials to develop new works. This led to the creation of a unique textile piece reflecting the transformation of the ship. What inspired me, as much as the vessel itself, was the enthusiasm, hard work and energy of the owners as they busily painted, scraped and fitted out the ship for its new life and, in doing so, gathered the support of local people, enthusiasts and advisors.

Päivi takes up the story:

The short note I found written on the title page of my copy of The Found Object in Textile Art *('Two ships that pass in the night – but speak the same "visual" language') perfectly describes the working relationship we have shared over the years. Long periods pass without our paths crossing but every time they do, we find ourselves deep in 'visual' conversation and exchange of ideas.*

When Gary and I acquired Light Vessel 21 in 2009 we had all the good intentions of documenting the unknown journey of transforming the historic ship from [being] the guiding light for mariners to her new role as a cultural beacon. Our vision was

Left Sketchbook pages of LV21 research, including fragments of the original paint rags and a transfer image on cloth.

Above The light vessel on location at the Gillingham Pier, Medway.

Right Shown on location on board the light vessel it is named after, this piece is in two sections and constructed from paint rags and pieces collected during the refurbishment of the vessel.

to dedicate some time throughout the restoration to create a continuous textile tapestry timeline and a digital archive of film and photos, combining our artistic practices, to chart this shared, life-changing new venture. But the reality of restoring a ship, the long hours of hard physical work, often covered in bitumen dust and paint, soon made us realize that this was an unrealistically ambitious plan.

As we had to put our own ideas of the artistic mapping of the restoration journey on hold, we were delighted when Cas approached us with her proposal to produce a new site-specific artwork inspired by LV21. She offered us an opportunity to gain an unbiased 'outsider's' view of our journey, and we loved the idea of Cas researching and visualizing an important period in the restoration of LV21, one that might otherwise have been completely missed.

It was fascinating to observe her methods of gathering materials for the piece on her site visits, from picking up

discarded paint rags and work gloves to collecting personal stories from the volunteers or noticing minute structural details on board LV21. The occasional glimpses of the work in progress gave us an insight into her fascinating working process.

The finished LV21 piece perfectly encapsulates a particular time and place in the history of the vessel and highlights elements that most matter to us. Small, hidden details and unexpected surprises, such as the reference to poppies, my favourite flower, offer another personal layer to the work.

Some of the most precious moments of the restoration are captured in the LV21 piece. And not only did Cas capture a part of our restoration journey though her work, [but] she also gave me the inspiration to get back to stitching and start work on that long-planned tapestry timeline.

Charting your course: the art of visual communication

Since embarking on her journey of nautical discovery in 2009 to restore the historic lightship LV21, turning the vessel into a cultural hub, Päivi has described herself as 'charting some unknown waters' while becoming hugely enthused by the rich maritime heritage. Fascinated by the vast array of visual aids used in marine communication and after several years of focusing on a career in arts management rather than developing her own artistic practice, she was suddenly engulfed by the need to return to her 'making' roots.

Flags have long played an important role for seafaring vessels. Flag signals allowed communication before the invention of radio and are still used – from semaphore and signal flags that send messages between ships or to shore, to flags showing nationality and ownership or which dress ships for ceremonial and festive occasions.

In flag semaphore, information is transmitted with hand-held flags, rods, disks, paddles, or occasionally bare or gloved hands. This international system of non-verbal communication (the current flag semaphore system at sea uses two short poles with square red and yellow flags) breaks language barriers and provides a fascinating way to spell out short messages and special meanings with various combinations of individual flags. Päivi's piece *Semaphore* explores this art of communication through subtle hints of its origins, incorporating a variety of recycled textiles and sea charts with hand and machine stitching to reveal a collection of keywords gathered from people who have, or have had, a connection with the lovingly restored LV21. The piece acts as a visual multilayered call sign, capturing particular moments in the past, present and future of LV21.

Above '*I wish to communicate with you*' = the letter K (dash, dot, dash in Morse code).

Left and right Päivi Seppälä, *Semaphore*, 2014. Works in progress. The stitched marks on wool fragments and rags collected from the vessel hint at the symbols used in semaphore and Morse-code communication. Semaphore was used to communicate and maintain personal messages during a busy life onboard. These pieces also echo the tradition of samplers as an exploration of process.

Päivi comments:

As a female 'captain' of Light Vessel 21, I also often come across the old sailors' superstition that women on board a ship equal bad luck. Descending from a long line of boat-builders, spending my youth sailing across the Baltic and now co-owning a historic lightship, it is no surprise that I strongly disagree with this traditional verse. My new work explores and rebels against this old belief by incorporating material elements that can be considered very feminine – silk fabric from a floral blouse, the hem of a maternity dress, fine lace, a vintage women's handkerchief …

While developing Semaphore, the movement of the traditional hand-held semaphore flags reminded me of the flutter of moths' wings as they fly around the ship's lantern, attracted by the light at night-time. The constant movement and shadow silhouettes etched against the bright light act as an imaginary communication between moth and man, wielding words using wings like semaphore flags as a code to signal personal messages and emotions. This similarity to semaphore, and the interaction between movement and light, threads through my work. I see the piece as metaphor for semaphore, a multilayered shorthand message, a time capsule harbouring a hidden story to be discovered …

The process of discovery

A playful investigative approach is a valid part of the design process. Allowing materials and the process of working to act as a trigger for your ideas leads to a more organic method of producing pieces. You may lose the visual perceptions of things you had in mind, but starting to play, or working blindly with a material, allows you to subconsciously respond to tactile and visual cues. Emotion, intuition and the process of discovery come into play. Work in partnership with a material to produce a range of objects, samples or 'things'. These can act as design tools for further development, as reflected upon by designer-maker Sheron King:

My working process involves the materiality of my workspace – I surround myself, wherever I work, with a variety of things, which to an onlooker may seem a clutter of gathered things in pots or baskets. I group the things that I have made together, rearrange, 'play' with, move into different groups and so on and so forth ... whilst all the time pondering, reflecting, conversing and eventually making design decisions. In this way, these things have communicated to me ... through a variety of senses and played roles in the forming of ideas. They have become a voice ...

Sheron fills her working environment with collections of fabrics, pretty objects, buttons and lace, and pieces evolve out of these collections. A series of paper and stitch neckpieces was started in response to a French postcard with a pretty woman on the front, addressed to a `Miss Nellie Darcy'.

Left and opposite Sheron King, *To Miss Nellie Darcy With Fondest Love*, 2012. Neckpieces, Wearable Art Forms collection.

Below Sheron King. The corner of the studio. Gathered buttons are meticulously ordered into old jam jars according to colour and type.

Pattern and form

Judith Shamp also talks about the role that play has in the composition of her pieces. Surface interest and organic pattern appeal to her precise way of organizing disparate elements, and she regularly employs a pattern based on a grid to get started. She teaches a form of focused drawing known as Zentangle, a meditational art form with clearly defined steps, named patterns and a teaching methodology. Judith affirms:

There is a universality in pattern exploration across the eons and among all cultures. In the gathering process, I work from an intuitive angle, pulling things out of my stash that look as though there is some commonality or pattern to them, be it colour, texture, or how the sheer layer of synthetic adds to the overall evolution of the work. I dwell in possibilities until I begin playing

with the shapes. My work often expresses itself through formal, symmetrical balance, and the interplay between organic and geometric shapes pulled me along that path.

Judith employs a broad range of techniques, working from vast collections of materials stored methodically. Using found objects, images, paper and fabrics, her methods of attachment vary accordingly. Many of her surfaces are built of sheers and tea-bag paper layered together and strengthened with gel medium.

Right Judith R Shamp, *The Zen of Tea*, 2003, 23 x 30 x 18cm (9 x 12 x 7in). Pleated tea-bag paper, recycled bamboo formed into a handle, various plastics, Shibori tape, beads and tea-bag tags.

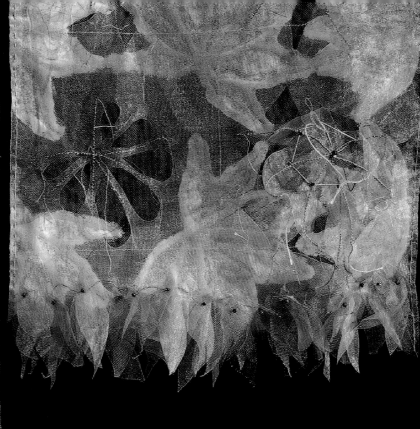

Above Judith R Shamp,
AkaHappa Kimono, 2009, 114 x
147cm (45 x 58in). Maple-
leaf shapes were cut with a
hot knife, leaving positive
and negative patterned
shapes. Small seed beads
give additional detail and
textures to the stitching.

Right Judith Shamp,
Different Strokes, 2012.
10 x 10cm (4 x 4in).
Zentangle patterns.

When working on free-hanging textile pieces, Judith uses a hot knife (a wood-burning tool) to layer and seal cut-out shapes of trimmed synthetic sheer fabrics. This prevents them fraying and melds one layer of sheer to another, keeping the pieces together until the hand stitching or machine stitching is done. The cutting with the hot knife is done against a strengthened glass or ceramic plate. These newly shaped, layered pieces are then applied to different types of fabrics with stitch. Please note that it is advisable to work in a room with an extractor fan and to wear a mask when burning or melting synthetic fabrics.

Judith remembers:

At the age of ten I was given my first kimono and this timeless garment has held my fascination from that day onward. Spying a variegated organza in fall colours at the Peter Jones Department store in London, I had to buy all that was left on the small roll. It reminded me of fall days in Indiana and again in Midland, Texas, where the only shade in our backyard was a maple tree. The brilliant fall colours connected me back to my Indiana years.

In the *The Zen of Tea*, Judith worked three-dimensionally, layering teabag paper over real Japanese teacups with gel medium to provide the cup forms. Tiny pleats in the teapot made with a smocking machine also added stability.

I loved the delicacy and deliberation given by Judith Shamp of Houston in her The Zen of Tea. *It's a tea set that's completely non-functional because it's made mostly of paper, tea labels and threads, with a garnish of beads. It can't be called miniature, but it's hardly hefty. You'd hate it if your cat decided to go after the fragile teapot made of tiny vertical accordion pleats of white rice paper.*

(ROBERTA BURNETT 2003)

Domestic tales

Nicola Flower is an artist living and working on a river lock in Maidstone, a place where the upper reaches of the tidal Medway meet the rest of the river. Her husband is the lock keeper and the sense of romanticism and history of this ancient waterway and its location inspire her creative process amongst the messiness of domestic life. She describes the influence of the environment:

In this place the tides go through you. We know the time of high and low tide each day and the position of the moon. For me the place has the heady combination of tough practical working environment mixed with history, English quaintness, old-fashioned slowness and stories – some true and some made up.

As a lecturer in art and design, Nicola enjoys working with other people and new situations. At home she is inquisitive and intuitive in her use of different mediums and often employs film, installation and ceramics, or whatever she feels is appropriate and effective in communicating her ideas. Her pieces always involve drawing, stitch, and textiles combined with found objects, the sourcing of which is by chance and always open to possibilities. She explains:

The romantic notions that the lock conjures up for me (imagine the traditional image of a lock cottage by the river) are in reality only snatched glimpses, as the day-to-day existence of being a mother, tutor and artist inevitably require me to adopt many roles at once (occasionally, in the role of artist, I reinforce the creative process by making the work 'in character'). To this end, my creative practice has become a case of directing my resources very carefully and being selective about where I invest my time. I have very real constraints that do not allow me to indulge my creativity beyond what has true meaning for me.

In common with many practitioners, Nicola has no designated workspace and describes having a 'nomadic existence', constantly moving around the house to work. Despite this she is determined that the work should not be compromised. Her family have had to learn to live with 'a piece of embroidery accompanying physics homework at the tea table'. This inevitably invites family discussion, and though not always welcome, it is a very useful process of review and assessment.

Nicola describes how her location infiltrates her work below:

Purses from the River Medway is inspired by my everyday observations and reflections at Allington Lock. They are a response to a shipwrecked handbag that I saw exhibited at the Museum of Bags and Purses in Amsterdam. I was intrigued by this salvaged object, so mundane and everyday, linked to the owner's identity, carrying with it her story, a familiar object, seemingly of little value and yet worth recovering from a shipwreck. I embroidered my personal stories of the lock on to

distressed and damaged purses, the stitches like drawn marks linking stories and memory to place. I then submerged the purses in the tidal River Medway, leaving them to distress and rust as though they had been lost or subjected to a harrowing experience, and so collecting in their linings a narrative forged from the effects of the ebb and flow of the tide at the lock. Stories stitched on the purses include images drawn from the surrounding woods and paths, objects we have unearthed in the garden and an armchair spinning down river at high tide.

Above Nicola Flower, *Purses from the River Medway*, 2012. Various sizes. Hand embroidery on to satin fabric.

Tales of loss

Jo Smith's work similarly tells a domestic tale. She uses a range of materials and experiments with ideas until she gets a mental picture of what she wants to do. In *Two Brothers, Three Sisters and a Mouse*, she talks about capturing the feeling of sorrow after the loss of family pets and treating her animal subjects like humans, creating little scenes to tell their story:

This work tells the tale of the loss, sorrow and suffering of the animals buried beneath the foliage at the bottom of the garden. Two rabbits, three kittens and a mouse.

The rabbits were the first family pets we had and our children's first experience of being carers and guardians of another living creature; they were much loved and sadly missed ... After numerous trips to the vet, they became gradually more and more ill. They wasted away before our very eyes; nothing could be done to save Twitch and Stripe.

The kittens were killed by fleas, victims of neglect at the hands of their carer; they were not properly looked after and their deaths were entirely preventable. They were due to come and live with us and just as they became old enough to leave their mother, one by one they began to keel over and die. Only one kitten out of a litter of five survived.

The mouse is the victim of one of our cats, and was dumped on the carpet.

The animal and human worlds have here been merged. There are portraits of the animals when they were happy and healthy, as we would have pictures of our loved ones upon the walls. Kittens' skeletons are stitched into the pattern in the doily, on to which the portraits are placed. Stitch drawings of the death of the kittens in their sleep show them on small beds surrounded by the fleas that killed them. The rabbits appear moth-eaten (these were constructed from forms made of newspaper and then covered with wire. The newspaper was burnt away after the form was achieved, and the wire then washed. Half-felted wool fibre was then attached to each of the wire skeletons.

Jo further comments:

There is barely a home in the land that has not been touched by grief and sorrow at the loss of a loved one. If nothing else, death serves to remind us how precious life is, no matter how small.

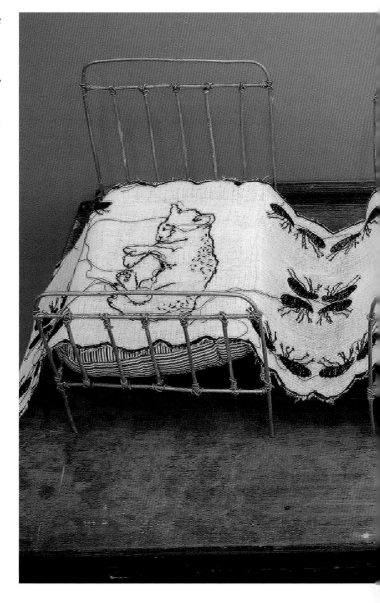

Right Jo Smith, *Two Brothers, Three Sisters and a Mouse* (detail), Hand-stitched kittens on white open-weave cloth on their hand-crafted beds.

Top Jo Smith, *Two Brothers, Three Sisters and a Mouse*, original installation, 2012. Showing the felted and wire forms of Twitch and Stitch on the left.

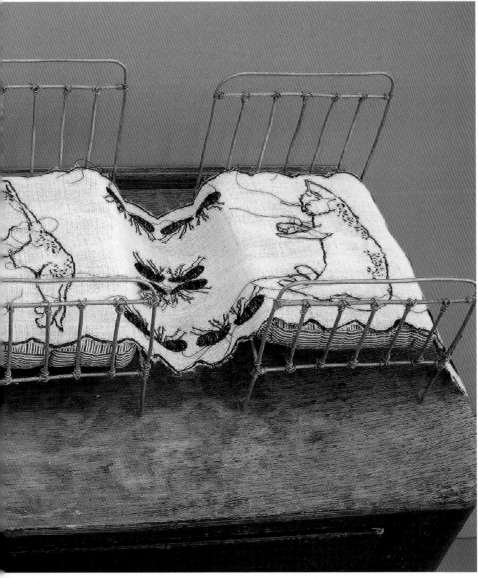

Bringing making and meaning together

Precious finds, mixed media and salvaged textiles are a wonderful resource for the textile artist. I have had the privilege of working with some amazing makers of all ages and abilities over the years, all of whom have helped to shape and inform my ideas. Sharing and exchange enables our ideas to grow and new stories to be told. My grandmother and father taught me to 'pay attention' and to never take the world around me for granted. My friends and colleagues, many of whom are represented in this book, demonstrate a wide application of creative practice.

Having the space and time to create and write is equally important, so thank you to my partner Derek, who quietly took up the slack when I needed to meet deadlines and did more than his fair share of the housework (and created a new space for me to work in).

With making comes meaning. The ways in which we explore the things that are meaningful to us come from our observations of and reflections on the world we live in. Our approach is individual and personal. It can be intense, multilayered, detailed, whimsical, organic or abstract. It can be anything. Textiles and the use of stitch are powerful tools for developing narrative. Stitch brings its own 'story' with it, enabling us to articulate a complex process of ideas, images, material and emotion.

Left *Shadow Grasses*, 2014. 15 x 15 x 50cm (6 x 6 x 20in). Transfer prints, stitch, dye and found cloth. I often make small works or books while travelling, or when I am pressed for time.

Glossary

analogous colours Colours that are adjacent to each other on the colour wheel. Yellows and oranges for example.

Bondaweb (Bondaweb 329, Wonder Under) An iron-on, fusible webbing with a non-stick paper backing, used for permanently bonding two fabrics together.

book form A book or book-like structure created as an original work of art, rather than a reproduction of a pre-existing book. Sometimes refered to as 'book art'.

boro Mended, patched and hand stitched Japanese textiles normally from the 19th-century.

Bubble Jet Set 2000 A liquid fabric treatment to pre-soak fabric making ink-jet-printed images washable. Some mediums such as Ink Aid can be applied with a brush.

complementary colours In colour theory complementary colours appear opposite each other on the colour wheel. The complementary of red is green (a mix of yellow and blue); the complementary of blue is orange (a mix of red and yellow); and the complementary of yellow is violet (a mix of red and blue).

conservation tissue A long-fibred tissue usually made from abaca hemp. Also referred to as archival interleaving tissue or wet-strength tissue. It is used for wrapping precious objects and for manuscript and book repairs.

cut-back appliqué Also referred to as reverse-appliqué in which the upper layers of cloth are cut away and turned back to expose the lower layers. The Molas made by the Kuna Indians of Panama are an example of this method.

dorukha The same stitch pattern as viewed from both sides of the cloth-making the fabric reversible.

dressmaker's carbon paper Paper with a coating of coloured wax or chalk on one or both sides. Used to transfer patterns or designs on to cloth.

drop cloth A piece of fabric (or plastic) that is put down while painting or printing to protect surfaces against dripping paint.

free-machine stitching Also referred to as free-motion stitching. Usually done with the attachment of a darning foot and with the feed dogs covered or lowered. This allows for free movement of the cloth which is normally stretched in an embroidery hoop.

gsm grams per square metre. The higher the gsm number, the heavier the paper.

heat press A machine which imprints a design on to a substrate, such as cloth with the application of heat and pressure. Normally associated with fabric use but can be applied to other products such as china, card puzzles and other products.

kantha A simple running stitch thought to have originated in Bangladesh and India as a means to sew discarded cloth together to make quilts, cushions and saris. The entire cloth is covered with beautiful motifs of flowers, animals, birds and geometrical shapes, as well as themes from everyday activities.

layout paper Thin, lightweight paper suitable for trying out ideas. Inexpensive and takes colour well.

long-arm quilter A specialist sewing machine used to sew together a quilt top, quilt batting and quilt backing into a finished quilt. These range from table-top machines for home use to industrial frame-mounted machines with large rollers on which the fabric layers are placed for quilting.

Lutradur A spunbonded nonwoven polyester fabric.

Markal Paintstiks Oil paint in a stick form. Can be used for painting, stencilling and fabric decoration. The paint can be used either straight from the stick or applied with a brush and heatset on fabric or air-cured on paper or card.

methyl cellulose A water-reversible adhesive that dries clear. The main ingredient in many wallpaper or conservation glues, it is also used as a binder in pastel crayons and in the fixation of delicate pieces of art as well as in book conservation.

mind-mapping A diagrammatic way or representing ideas, words and observations around a central word or theme.

monofilament thread Nylon clear 'invisible' thread used for quilting and sewing.

mordant A chemical binding agent to set dyes on fabrics.

nakshi kantha A type of embroidered quilt, typical of the centuries-old Bengali art tradition in Bangladesh and West Bengal, India. The Bengali word 'naksha' refers to the elaborate embroidered artistic patterns.

sashiko A form of decorative reinforcement stitching (or functional embroidery) from Japan. Sashiko literally means 'little stabs' and is a type of running stitch technique traditionally used, often in boro.

thermofax A screen created using a thermofax machine, an old photocopy technology. An image is burned into the screen to create a lightweight screen capable of printing the same image hundreds of times.

Tissuetex A strong, wet-strength tissue which can be dyed or painted, stitched or laminated to itself or other papers or fabrics, using cellulose paste or glue (see conservation tissue).

viewfinder A viewfinder normally refers to the frame a photographer looks through to compose a picture. It also refers to L-shaped frames to isolate a chosen area of an image or design and pulling it out as an abstract for further development.

Zentangle An abstract drawing created using repetitive patterns according to the trademarked Zentangle Method.

Bibliography

Barton, Serena, *Wabi-Sabi Art Workshop: Mixed-Media for Embracing Imperfection and Celebrating Happy Accidents* (North Light Books, 2013).

Bourgouis, Louise, quote taken from gallery publication, Hauser & Wirth, 2010.

Burnett, Roberta, Artists create 'Tea Party' in many mediums, *The Arizona Republic Newspaper*, September 12, 2003 by Roberta Burnett in reference to the exhibition '*Steeped in Tradition, The Contemporary Art of Tea II* Mesa Contemporary Arts.

Cocker, Mark, *Crow Country* (Jonathan Cape, 2007). Reproduced by permission of The Random House Group Limited.

Cohen, Leonard, quote taken from an interview published in *Montreal Globe and Mail*, May 2007.

Digby, John and Joan, *The Collage Handbook* (Thames & Hudson, 1985).

Elinor, Gillian, *Women and Craft* (Virago Press, 1987)

Flint, India, *Eco Colour: Botanical Dyes for Beautiful Textiles* (Murdoch Books, 2008).

Greenlees, Kay, *Creating Sketchbooks for Embroiderers and Textile Artists* (Batsford, 2003).

Hardesty, Pamela, Original project brief for 'Things/Daiktai' and the resulting exhibition at CIT Wandesford Quay Gallery, Cork, 2014.

Hill, June, 'Domestic Goddess', *Embroidery*, May/June 2014.

Holmes, Cas, *The Found Object in Textile Art* (Batsford, 2010).

Holmes, Cas and Anne Kelly, *Connected Cloth* (Batsford, 2013).

Holmes, Val, *Collage, Stitch , Print* (Batsford, 2012)

Hopper, John, 'The Edgelands of Cas Holmes.' *Fiber Art Magazine* 4 (2) (fall 2014): 28.

Howard, Constance*, The Constance Howard Book of Stitch* (Batsford, 1979)

Hurlstone, Nigel, quoted in Alice Kettle and Jane McKeating, *Drawing and the Chimera of Embroidery: Machine Stitch Perspectives* (A&C Black, 2010).

Impey, Sara, *Text in Textile Art* (Batsford, 2013)

James, Rosie, *Stitch Draw* (Batsford, 2014).

Jones, Dan, 'Fabric of Britain: The Wonder of Embroidery', BBC4. *Handmade in Britain* series. Broadcast October 2013.

King, Miles, *England's Green Unpleasant Land*? (Plantlife, 2012). Available online: http://www.plantlife.org.uk/publications/ englands_green_unpleasant_land (accessed December 2014).

Laury, Jean Ray, *The Photo Transfer Handbook: Snap It, Print It, Stitch It* (C&T Publishing, 2011).

Meech, Sandra, *Connecting Art to Stitch* (Batsford, 2009).

Millar, Lesley. 2012, *Cloth and Memory 1*', Exhibition catalogue: Salts Mill, Yorkshire (Direct Design Books, 2012).

Niffenegger, Audrey, *The Time Traveler's Wife* (MacAdam/Cage, 2003). Reprinted by the permission of Regal Literary, Inc. as agent for the author. Copyright © Audrey Niffenegger.

Parker, Rozsika, *The Subversive Stitch* (The Women's Press, 1984)

Parrott, Helen, *Mark-Making in Textile Art* (Batsford, 2013)

Pryor, Greg, *Holly story – look both ways* [online]. Artlink, Vol. 33, No. 1, Mar 2013.

Prichard, Sue, 'The TechnoCraft Collection', Neil Bottle: Ruthin Craft Centre Retail Gallery Focus, September 2010.

Prichard, Sue, *Quilts 1700–2012* (V&A Publishing, 2010)

Schwarz, Tilleke, *Mark Making* (Ter Burg, Offset 2008)

Schoeser, Mary, *Textiles: The Art of Mankind* (Thames & Hudson, 2012)

Thittichai, Kim, *Reclaimed Textiles* (Batsford, 2013)

Wandersee, J., and E. Schussler, *Plant Science Bulletin* 47 (1998), Botanical Society of America, Inc.

Yang, Sunny and Rochelle M. Narsin, *Textile Art of Japan* (Japan Publications Trading Co, 2011)

Websites and Suppliers

Artists' websites

Jane LaFazio – janelafazio.com

Tania McCormack – cargocollective.com/taniamccormack

Dionne Swift – dionneswift.co.uk

Mary Fisher – maryfisher.com

Cork CIT – arts.cit.ie

Jeanette Appleton – jeanetteappletonuk.wixsite.com/mysite

Yoriko Yoneyama – yorikoyoneyama.jimdo.com

Rosalind Wyatt – rosalindwyatt.com

Noriko Endo – norikoendo.com

Holly Story – hollystory.com

Christine Atkins – christineatkins.com.au

Anne Kelly – annekellytextiles.com

Rosalind Davis – rosalinddavis.co.uk

Neil Bottle – neilbottle.com

Peta Lloyd – arthives.com/petalloyd

Niru Reid – nirureid.co.uk

Sheilagh Dyson – @SheilaghDysonArtist

Rosie James – rosiejames.com

Rachael Howard – 62group.org.uk/artist/rachael-howard

Tilleke Schwarz – tillekeschwarz.com

Kirsty Whitlock – kirstywhitlock.com

James Hunting – jameshunting.com

Päivi Seppälä – lv21.co.uk

Sheron King – madhattersstudio.com

Judith Shamp – narrative-threads.com

Mandy Pattulo – mandypattullo.co.uk

Nicola Flower – nicolaflower.co.uk

Jo Smith – josmithtextileartist.wordpress.com

Ezzter Bornemisza – bornemisza.com

Alke Schmidt – alkeschmidt.com

Cas Holmes – casholmes.co.uk, casholmes.uk

Websites

www.textileartist.org
An excellent website with links to embroidery groups, suppliers and exhibitions

wowbook.d4daisy.com

www.texi.org
The Textile Institute

www.cowslipworkshops.co.uk

www.thequiltersguild.org.uk,
The Quilters' Guild of the United Kingdom

www.embroderersguild.com
The Embroiderers' Guild

www.royal-needlework.org.uk
Royal School of Needlework

www.canadianquilter.com
Canadian Quilters' Association

www.62group.org.uk
Contemporary British textile arts group

www.westdean.org.uk
Courses in textiles and other subjects

www.quiltart.eu
Quilt Art group

www.twistedthread.com
Festival of Quilts and Knitting and Stitching Shows UK

www.transitionandinfluence.com
Contemporary textile arts practice including Cloth and Memory exhibition

www.scotlandstapestry.com
The Great Tapestry of Scotland

www.wabisabiart.blogspot.com
Site about Japanese aesthetics

www.thesketchbookchallenge.com

www.zentangle.com

www.sashiko.org.uk

Museums and places to visit

www.moda.mdx.ac.uk
Museum of Design and Architecture, Middlesex University

www.gardenmuseum.org.uk
Garden Museum

www.wmgallery.org.uk
William Morris Gallery
www.vam.ac.uk
Victoria and Albert Museum

www.warnertextilearchive.co.uk
Museum and textile research archive

www.nationaltrust.org
Gardens, parks and houses throughout the UK

www.plantlife.org
Reserves throughout the UK

www.vam.ac.uk
Victoria and Albert Museum

www.thetextileblog.blogspot.co.uk
Current textiles and creative practice

www.nationaltrust.org
Gardens, parks and houses throughout the UK

www.plantlife.org
Reserves throughout the UK

Suppliers

Explore your local hardware and 'Do It Yourself' shops for paint, glues, fittings and equipment.
Local art and hobby shops, supermarkets, charity and second-hand shops are full of wonderful alternative stuff to work with. Accept gifts or donations of materials from friends and colleagues –you never what you might find to use and share in the 'gift' and what new project it could lead to. Re-use where possible.

George Weil & Sons
Fibrecrafts and many other brands
Old Portsmouth Road
Peasmarsh
Guildford GU3 1LZ
Surrey
Tel: 01483 565800
www.georgeweil.com

Rainbow Silks
6 Wheelers Yard, High Street, Great Missenden, Buckinghamshire HP16 OAL
Tel:01494 862111
www.rainbowsilks.co.uk

Whaleys (Bradford) Ltd
Tel:01274 521309
www.whaleys-bradford.ltd.uk

Woven Monkey, Digital printing on fabric.
Unit 2. Winster Park, Corporation Road, Ilkeston, Derbyshire, DE7 4BN
0115 9301837
www.wovenmonkey.com

General art supplies

Colourcraft (C &A) Ltd (manufacturer of Dyes, Fabric Paints and Brusho and distributors of a wide range of materials including Markal Paintstiks and Koh-I-Noor)
Unit 5, 555 Carlisle Street, Sheffield S4 8DT
Tel: 0114 2421431
www.colourcraftltd.com

Great Art
1 Nether Street, Alton, Hants GU34 1EU
Tel: 01420 593333
www.greatart.co.uk

USA and Canada
Pro Chemical and Dye Inc.
Tel: 800 228 9393
www.prochemical.com
Dharma Trading Company
Tel: 800 542 5227
www.dharmatrading.com

Quilting Daily
www.quiltingdaily.com

eQuilter
Largest selection of quilting fabrics, free quilt patterns
6201 Spine Road, Suite A,
Boulder, Colorado 80301 USA
www.equilter.com

Australia
The Thread Studio
www.thethreadstudio.com

Index

Acknowledgements and Picture credits

All by Jacqui Hurst except the following: pp.5,10,15,16 (bottom), 18 (bottom two images), 19, 20,21 22 (top left), 27 (right), 29 (bottom), 30 (top), 40, 47 (middle) 51, 54, 58 (right) 66, 67, 80 (top) 84, 90, 104, 107 Cas Holmes; 4, 24,34, 35, 43 (bottom) Things/ Daiktai, CIT Crawford College of Art and Design and Wandesford Quay Gallery, Cork; 6 Alex Hewitt; 7 © V&A Museum, London;14,59,60; Ann Somerset Miles; 23 Tania McCormack; 27, (left two) Museum of Domestic Design and Architecture, Middlesex University; 30, 31 (bottom) Dionne Swift; 36 Gerry Diebel; 37 Susan Crowe; 45 Rob Kennard; 52 Noriko Endo; 58 (left) Art Van Go; 61,62 Robert Frith; 64,73,108 Neil Bottle; 68,69 Christine Atkins; 70 Anne Kelly; 71 Rosalind Davis; 72 Eszter Bornemisza; 76,77 Peta Lloyd; 79 Niru Reid; 83 Alke Schmidt; 88,89 Sheilagh Dyson; 91 Rosie James; 92 Rachael Howard; 93 Mary Fisher Productions, Inc.; 94,95 Kirsty Whitlock; 96,105 Mandy Pattullo; 98 Tilleke Schwarz; 100 Rosalind Wyatt; 102 James Hunting; 110,111 Gary Weston; 112,113 Päivi Seppälä; 114,115 Sheron King; 116 Mike McCormick; 117 Judith R Shamp; 118,119 Nicola Flower; 120,121 Jo Smith.

The author would like to thank the following:
Organizations and named artists listed in the text, for use and creation of images and text. Arts organizations, colleges and sponsors mentioned in the text who continue to support many of the exhibitions and projects mentioned in the text; The Batsford team: my editor Lucy Smith and designers Elizabeth Healey and Michelle Mac for the wonderful work on this book; Jacqui Hurst for her excellent photography; Friends and family for their patience, feedback and advice.